United States
Department of
Agriculture

Forest
Service

Northern
Research Station

Resource Bulletin
NRS-39

PULPWOOD PRODUCTION IN THE NORTHERN REGION, 2006

Ronald J. Piva

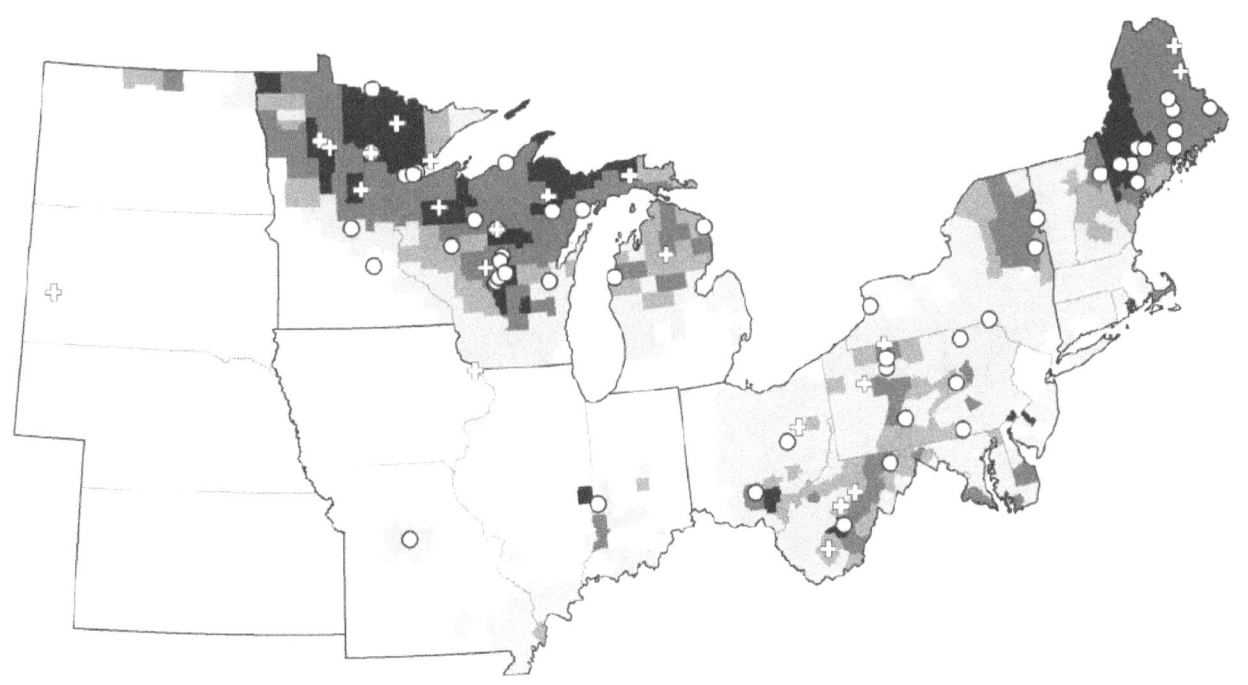

Abstract

Discusses 2006 production and receipts of pulpwood in the Northern Region. Breaks down production from four subregions: Central States, Lake States, Mid-Atlantic States, and New England States, by species group for each state and compares production with that of previous years. Production for 2006 for the Plains States by species group and product form are included.

The Author

Ronald J. Piva, Forester, received a B.S. in forest management from the University of Missouri-Columbia. He joined the Forest Service in 1987 and has been working with the Northern Research Station's Forest Inventory and Analysis unit since.

Manuscript received for publication November 2009

CONTENTS

INTRODUCTION

Current detailed information about pulpwood production[1] is necessary for intelligent planning and decisionmaking in wood procurement, forest-resource management, forest-industry development, and scientific studies.

This report includes information regarding pulpwood produced for use in the manufacture of all primary products made from reconstituted wood fiber. The two major products produced from pulpwood are pulp products and composite panel products. Pulp products include wood pulp, corrugated medium, roofing material, and insulation board. Composite panel products include flakeboard, waferboard, medium density fiberboard, hardboard, particleboard, oriented strandboard, and parallel strand lumber. Wood chips or fibers used at composite panel mills are nearly identical to wood chips or fibers used at pulp mills. Therefore, including this wood in our data compilation provides a more accurate estimate of demand for pulpwood-like material. This report presents the production of the raw fiber material delivered to mills. Thus, these data report only that portion of the timber harvest used as raw material and do not necessarily reflect the volume of growing stock harvested.

Pulpwood is a large component of the industrial timber products harvested annually in the Northern Region, accounting for more than half of the total harvest in some states each year. The Central States (Illinois, Indiana, Iowa, Missouri), Lake States (Michigan, Minnesota, Wisconsin), Mid-Atlantic States (Delaware, Maryland, New Jersey, New York, Ohio, Pennsylvania, West Virginia), New England States (Connecticut, Maine, Massachusetts, New Hampshire, Rhode Island, Vermont), and Plains States (Kansas, Nebraska, North Dakota, South Dakota) are discussed separately because the timber types in each area are different and the flow of wood between the areas is nominal. Results for pulpwood production and receipts are discussed at the broad regional level to avoid revealing the operations of individual mills.

---

[1]Definitions of many terms used in this publication are found in the "Definition of Terms" section found in the Appendix.

STUDY METHODS

The Northern Research Station's (NRS) pulpwood study uses questionnaires designed to determine the size and composition of the primary pulpwood-using industry, its use of roundwood and wood residues, and its generation and disposition of wood residues. These questionnaires were mailed or emailed to all known users of pulpwood in the Northern Region, and to all Canadian pulpwood mills that were possible users of Northern Region pulpwood. Follow-up emails and phone calls were made in an effort to achieve a 100 percent response. Completed questionnaires were sent to NRS for data entry and processing.

As part of data entry and processing, all roundwood volumes reported on the questionnaires were converted to standard units of measure using regional conversion factors found in the Appendix. Timber removals by source of material and harvest residues generated during logging were estimated from standard product volumes using factors developed from logging utilization studies previously conducted by NRS. Finalized data on NRS's pulpwood receipts were loaded into a regional timber removals database where they were supplemented with data from other regions to provide a complete assessment of the Northern Region's production and use of pulpwood. Table 30 lists the pulpwood mills from Canada and other regions that reported receiving pulpwood from the Northern Region.

As part of requirements for reporting forest resource statistics for the national Resource Planning Act (RPA), the Northern Station must provide harvest volumes by state, county, and species. Some mills are not able to provide the county and/or species level of reporting. Instead, they report species volume as different groups, such as mixed hardwoods and softwoods, or county volumes listed as other counties instead of specific. In such cases, volumes are prorated to counties and/or species based on distance from mill and Forest Inventory and Analysis statistics of the volume of growing stock on forest land by county and species.

In 2006, surveys were conducted with pulp and composite panel mills from the Northern Region. Mills reported pulpwood receipts by species group and county of origin. This bulletin presents the results of the survey, compiles the data, compares results with those of 2005 and earlier years, and discusses trends in pulpwood production and use.

When new surveys are completed, errors and omissions from previous surveys are corrected. As a result of ongoing efforts to improve the survey's efficiency and reliability, changes may have been made to the previous survey's data. All comparisons and analyses in this report are based on the reprocessed data from earlier surveys, which may vary slightly from previously published data.

CENTRAL STATES

PRODUCTION AND RECEIPTS

Because of few pulpwood mills in the Central States, detailed county and receipt information is not reported for Illinois, Indiana, Iowa, and Missouri to avoid disclosure of information from individual mills.

- There were 398,000 cords of pulpwood produced in the Central States in 2006. Overall, 20 percent came from roundwood (including chips from roundwood) and 80 percent came from the residue of wood-using plants (Fig. 1 and Table 1).

- Hard hardwoods was the most harvested species group for pulpwood with 55,000 cords (70 percent of the total roundwood harvested) (Table 2). Another 18,000 cords of soft hardwoods (23 percent of the total roundwood harvest) and 6,000 cords of softwoods (7 percent of the total roundwood harvested) were harvested in 2006.

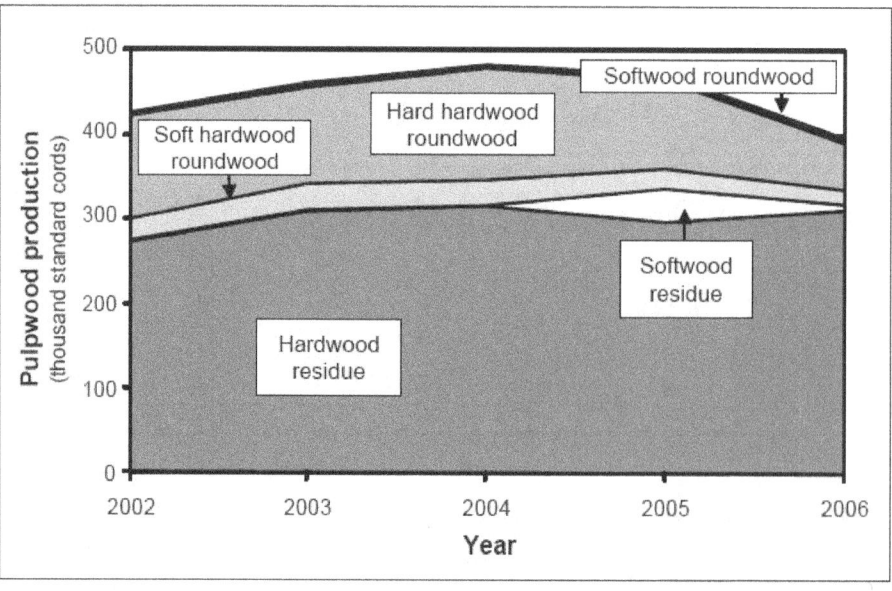

Figure 1.—Pulpwood production in the Central States by softwoods, hard hardwoods, soft hardwoods, and roundwood and residues, 2002-2006.

4

- Missouri was the largest producer of pulpwood in the Central States in 2006 with 52 percent of the regional total, or 207,000 cords. Indiana produced 39 percent of the pulpwood produced in the Central States, Illinois produced 6 percent, and Iowa produced 3 percent (Fig. 2).

- Almost 90 percent of the Central State's pulpwood production went to mills that produce pulp products. All of the roundwood harvested for pulpwood and 98 percent of the mill residues used for pulpwood were used by pulp mills (Fig. 3).

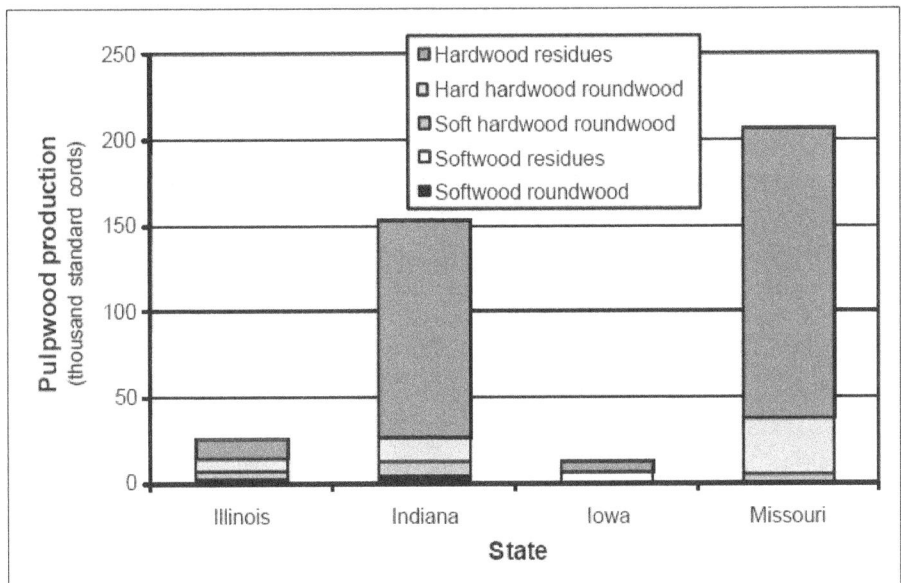

Figure 2.—Pulpwood production in the Central States by state, softwoods, hard hardwoods, soft hardwoods, and product form, 2006.

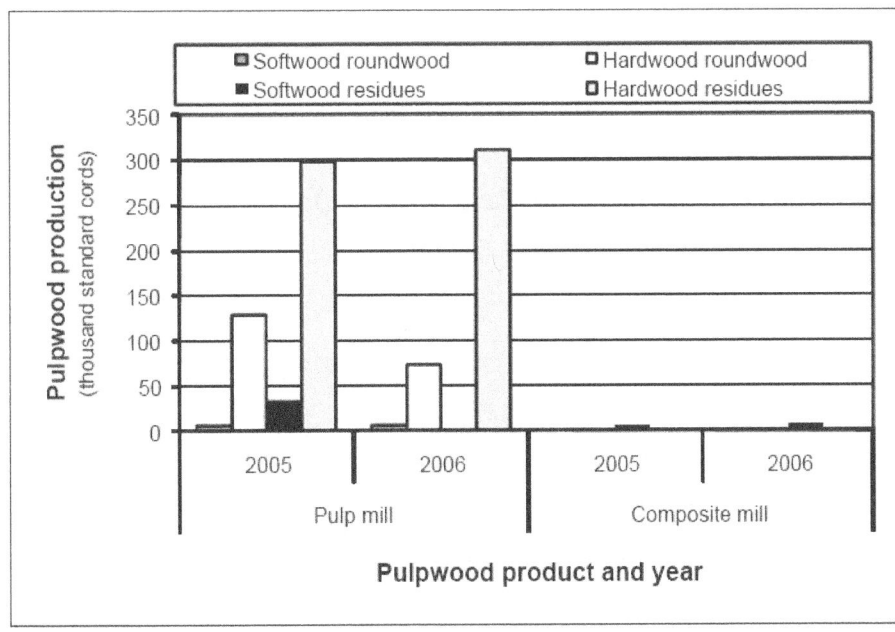

Figure 3.—Pulpwood production in the Central States by softwood and hardwood, product form, and mill type, 2005 and 2006.

- Central States pulpwood mills received 87,000 cords of pulpwood in 2006. Twenty-two percent of the pulpwood received was in the form of roundwood. The remainder was residues from other primary wood processors. The Lake States supplied 20 percent of the pulpwood (all residues from other primary wood processors) to mills in the Central States.

INDUSTRY TRENDS AND ANALYSIS

- Pulpwood production in the Central States decreased by 16 percent, from 473,000 cords in 2005 to 398,000 cords in 2006. Pulpwood production from mill residues decreased by 5 percent and pulpwood production from roundwood decreased by 42 percent.

- Only 4 percent of the roundwood and 16 percent of the mill residues that were produced in the Central States for pulpwood went to mills in the Central States. Mills in the Southern States received 77 percent of the total wood material produced in the Central States for pulpwood in 2006. Collectively, the Lake States and Mid-Atlantic States received 6 percent.

- In 2006, there were two pulp mills and one composite panel mill in the Central States (Table 3). The International Paper mill at Fort Madison, Iowa, closed at the end of 2005.

- Pulpwood harvesting in most of the Central States was minimal in 2006. There were 50 counties in the Central States that had pulpwood harvesting. There was an average of 17 cords of pulpwood harvested per thousand acres of timberland from these 50 counties. Only three counties had pulpwood harvest greater than 75 cords per thousand acres of timberland (Fig. 4).

- Pulpwood production for the Central States is expected to decrease again in 2007 as pulp products markets continued to decline. Also, the International Paper mill at Terre Haute, Indiana, closed in October 2007.

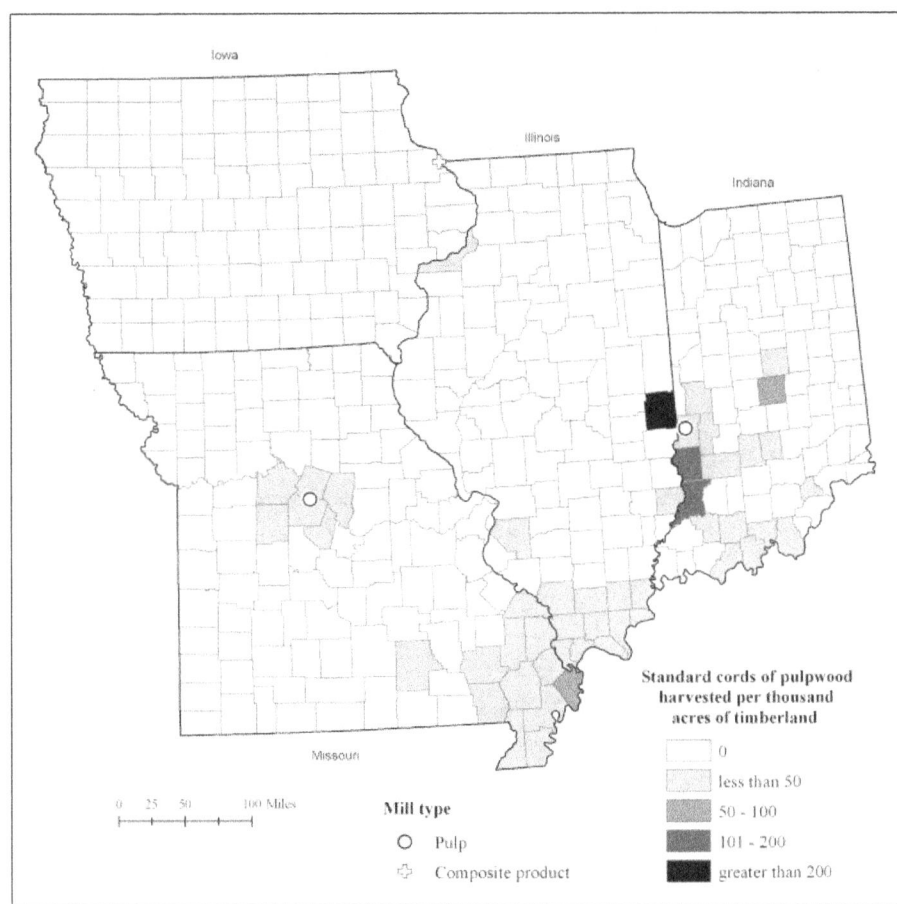

Figure 4.—Standard cords of pulpwood harvested per thousand acres of timberland in the Central States by county, 2006. Area of timberland is based on U.S. Forest Service Inventory and Analysis data for 2006. Map shows active pulp and composite products mills. See Table 3 for pulpwood mills in the Central States.

LAKE STATES

PRODUCTION

- Pulpwood production in the Lakes States fell from 9.8 million cords in 2005 to 7.7 million cords in 2006, a 22 percent decrease. In 2006, 87 percent of the pulpwood produced came from roundwood and 13 percent were mill residues from other primary wood processors in the Lake States (Table 4).

- Aspen/balsam poplar remained the dominant species group harvested for pulpwood in the Lake States in 2006 with 3.0 million cords, or 44 percent of the total roundwood. Other important species harvested for pulpwood in 2006 were soft maple (766,000 cords), hard maple (650,000 cords), spruce (334,000 cords), and balsam fir (288,000 cords) (Fig. 5 and Table 5).

- Production was fairly evenly divided between the three Lake States. Minnesota replaced Wisconsin as the leading producer of pulpwood in the Lake States in 2006 with 2.7 million cords. Wisconsin and Michigan each produced 2.5 million cords of pulpwood in 2006 (Fig. 6).

- Over two-thirds (5.2 million cords) of the pulpwood produced in the Lake States went to pulp mills. The remaining 2.5 million cords of pulpwood produced went to composite products mills (Table 6).

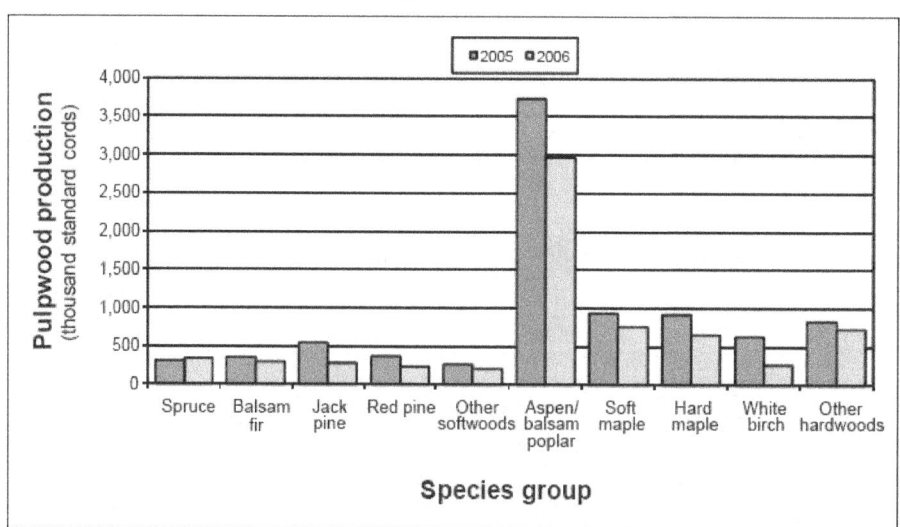

Figure 5.—Pulpwood production from roundwood in the Lake States by species group, 2005 and 2006.

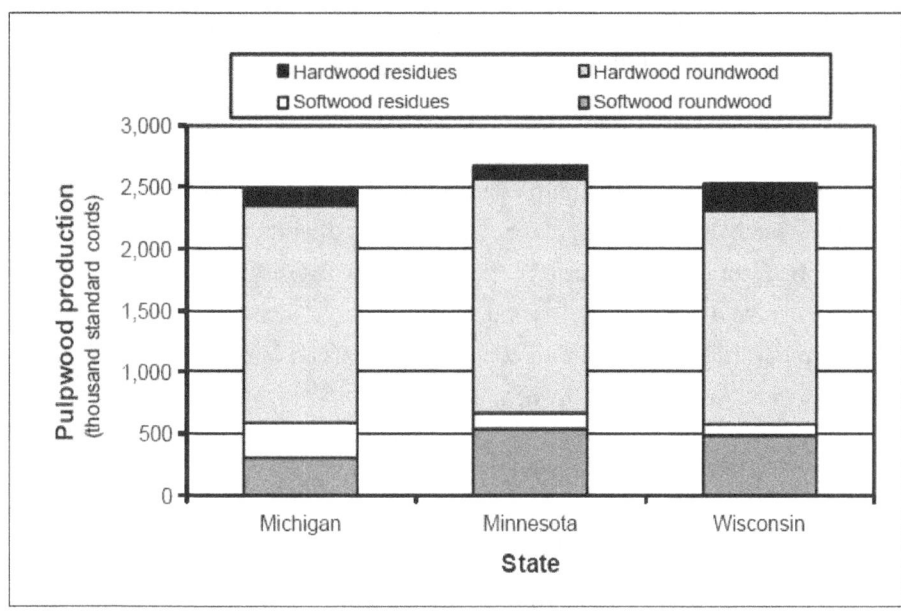

Figure 6.—Pulpwood production in the Lake States by state, softwood and hardwood, and product form, 2006.

- The production of pulpwood decreased by 21 percent for pulp products and 23 percent for composite products between 2005 and 2006 (Fig. 7 and Table 7).

RECEIPTS

- In 2006, 20 pulp and 16 composite products mills in the Lake States acquired 7.8 million cords of pulpwood, a decrease of 24 percent from the year before.

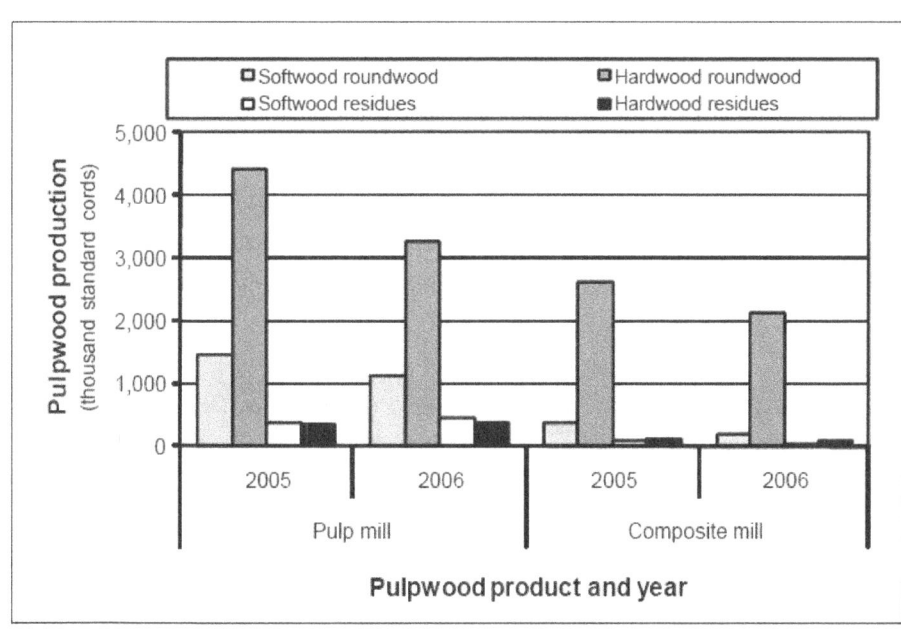

Figure 7.—Pulpwood production in the Lake States by softwood and hardwood, product form, and mill type, 2006.

9

- Pulpwood mills in Minnesota processed 40 percent of the total receipts in the Lake States; Michigan processed 32 percent; and Wisconsin processed 28 percent.

- Almost 99 percent of the pulpwood produced in the Lake States was processed by mills in the Lake States. Pulpwood produced in the Lake States supplied just over 96 percent of the total wood material required by Lake States mills. Imports of pulpwood material from Canada provided another 3 percent. The remaining 1 percent of the pulpwood imported by Lake States mills came from Illinois, Iowa, and North Dakota.

INDUSTRY TRENDS AND ANALYSIS

- Lake States pulpwood production from roundwood decreased by 24 percent from 2005 to 2006, while pulpwood production from mill residues increased by 4 percent.

- Almost 80 percent of the roundwood harvested for pulpwood in the Lake States occurred in the northern tier of Forest Inventory Units (Eastern Upper Peninsula and Western Upper Peninsula Units of Michigan, Aspen-Birch and Northern Pine Units of Minnesota, and Northeastern and Northwestern Units of Wisconsin) (Tables 8, 9, and 10).

- There were 171 counties in the Lake States that had pulpwood harvesting, with an average of 139 cords of pulpwood harvested per thousand acres of timberland. Forty-five counties had pulpwood harvest levels greater than 150 cords per thousand acres of timberland (Fig. 8).

- Michigan and Wisconsin were hard hit by mill closures in 2005 and 2006. In 2005, idled or closed mills included: GFP Strandwood Corp., Hancock, MI; Menasha Packaging Co., Inc., Otsego, MI; Sappi Fine Paper, Muskegon, MI; Rodman Industries, Marinette, WI; Smart Papers, LLC (Fraser Paper, Inc.), Park Falls, WI; Wausau Paper, Brokaw, WI. In 2006, Georgia-Pacific Corp., Gaylord, MI, and Ainsworth Engineered (USA), LLC, Grand Rapids, MN, were also idled or closed.

- Pulpwood production for the Lake States was expected to decrease again in 2007 as pulp products and composite products markets continued to decline. Three more mills were closed or idled in 2007: Ainsworth Engineered (USA), LLC, Cook, MN; CertainTeed Corp., Shakopee, MN; Trus Joist by Weyerhaeuser, Deerwood, MN.

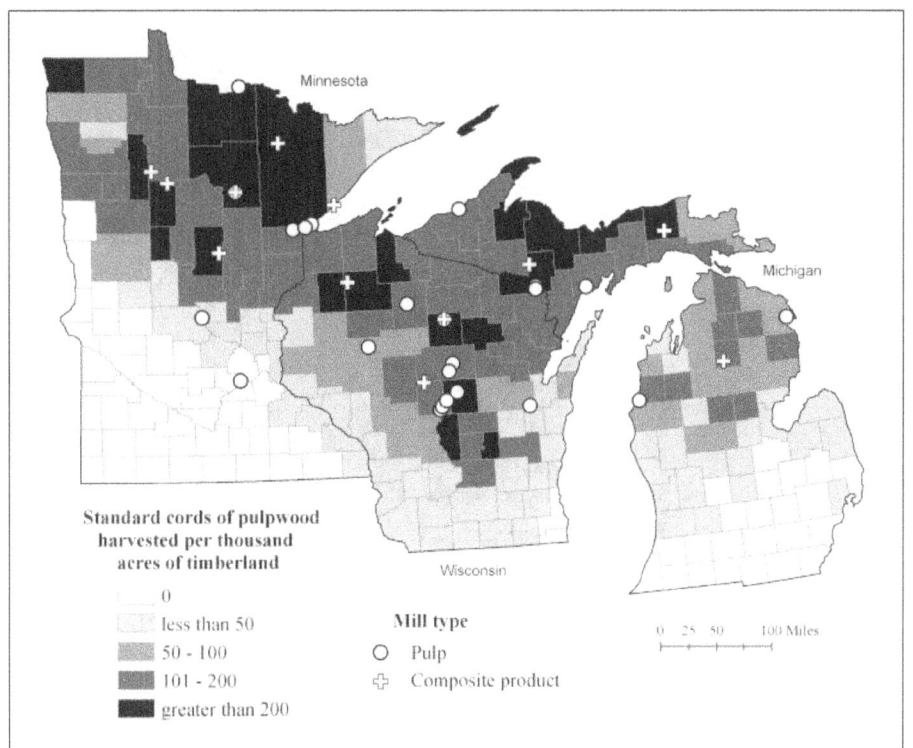

Figure 8.—Standard cords of pulpwood harvested per thousand acres of timberland in the Lake States by county, 2006. Area of timberland is based on U.S. Forest Service Inventory and Analysis data for 2006. Map shows active pulp and composite products mills. See Table 11 for pulpwood mills in the Lake States.

MID-ATLANTIC STATES

PRODUCTION

- Pulpwood production in the Mid-Atlantic States increased 4 percent, from 4.1 million cords in 2005 to 4.2 million cords in 2006. In 2006, 63 percent of the pulpwood produced came from roundwood and 37 percent came from mill residues from other primary wood processors in the Mid-Atlantic States (Table 12).

- Soft maple and yellow-poplar accounted for almost 30 percent of the total volume harvested for pulpwood in the Mid-Atlantic States in 2006, with 397,000 cords and 364,000 cords, respectively. Other important species harvested for pulpwood in 2006 were hard maple (209,000 cords), white oaks (195,000 cords), red oaks (182,000 cords), and white pine (173,000 cords) (Fig. 9 and Table 13).

- Almost one-third (1.4 million cords) of the pulpwood produced in the Mid-Atlantic States came from Pennsylvania. West Virginia was the second largest producer of pulpwood with 1.2 million cords (Fig. 10).

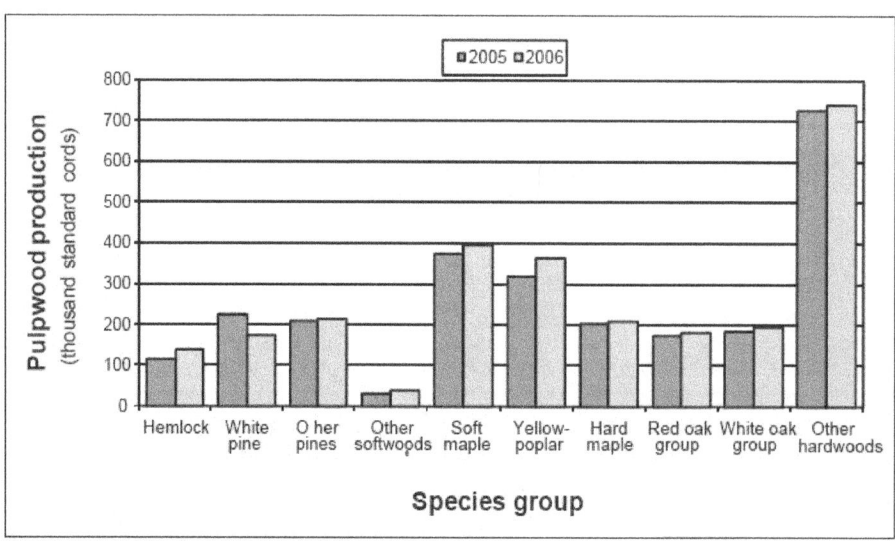

Figure 9.—Pulpwood production in the Mid-Atlantic States by species group, 2005 and 2006.

12

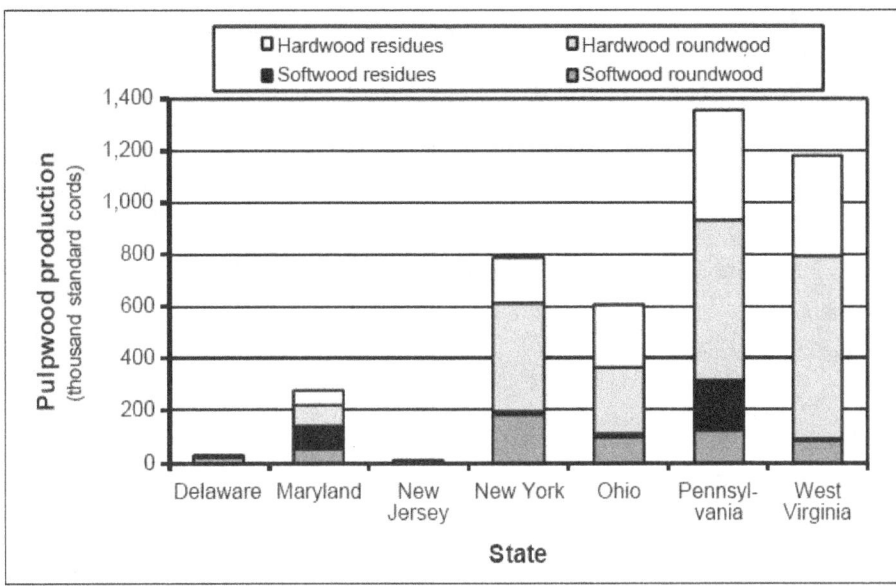

Figure 10.—Pulpwood production in the Mid-Atlantic States by state, softwood and hardwood, and product form, 2006.

- Pulp mills received almost 70 percent (2.9 million cords) of the pulpwood produced in the Mid-Atlantic States. The remaining 1.3 million cords of pulpwood produced went to composite products mills (Table 14).

- The production of pulpwood for composite products increased by 12 percent from 2005 to 2006, while production of pulpwood for pulp products remained at the 2005 level (Fig. 11 and Table 15).

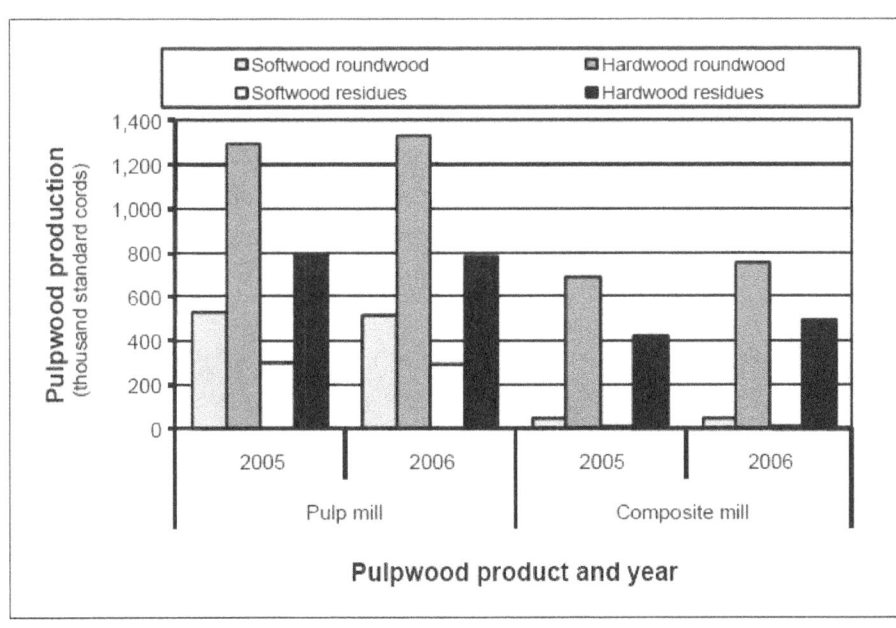

Figure 11.—Pulpwood production in the Mid-Atlantic States by softwood and hardwood, product form, and mill type, 2006.

RECEIPTS

Because of few pulpwood mills in Delaware, Maryland, and New Jersey, detailed receipt information is not reported for the Mid-Atlantic States to avoid disclosure of information from individual mills.

- In 2005, nine wood pulp and 12 composite products mills in the Mid-Atlantic States acquired 4.2 million cords of pulpwood, an increase of 6 percent from the year before.

- Pulpwood mills in Pennsylvania processed more than one-third of the total receipts in the Mid-Atlantic States.

- Eighty-seven percent of the pulpwood produced in the Mid-Atlantic States was processed by mills in the Mid-Atlantic States. Southern States supplied 72 percent, and New England States supplied 24 percent of pulpwood that was imported into the Mid-Atlantic States. The remaining 4 percent of pulpwood imports came from the Central States and Canada.

INDUSTRY TRENDS AND ANALYSIS

- Pulpwood production in the Mid-Atlantic States increased by 4 percent for both roundwood and mill residues.

- Roundwood harvested for pulpwood occurred in 261 of the 320 counties in the Mid-Atlantic States (Tables 16, 17, 18, 19, and 20). One-quarter of the total harvest came from only nine counties: New York—Essex, Franklin, St. Lawrence, and Saratoga counties; Pennsylvania—Clearfield and McKean counties; West Virginia—Greenbrier, Nicholas, and Randolph counties.

- An average of 50 cords of pulpwood was harvested per thousand acres of timberland from the 261 counties in the Mid-Atlantic States that harvested pulpwood in 2006. Thirty-two counties had pulpwood harvest greater than 100 cords per thousand acres of timberland (Fig. 12).

- No pulpwood mills closed in the Mid-Atlantic States in 2005, 2006, or 2007. Since the 2001 pulpwood report for the Northeast (Baker et al. 2005), the International Paper mills in Corinth, NY, and Erie, PA, were closed in 2002.

- A small decrease was expected in 2007 as pulp product and composite product markets continued to decline. Pulpwood mill closings in the New England States will have a minor effect on the production of pulpwood from Mid-Atlantic States.

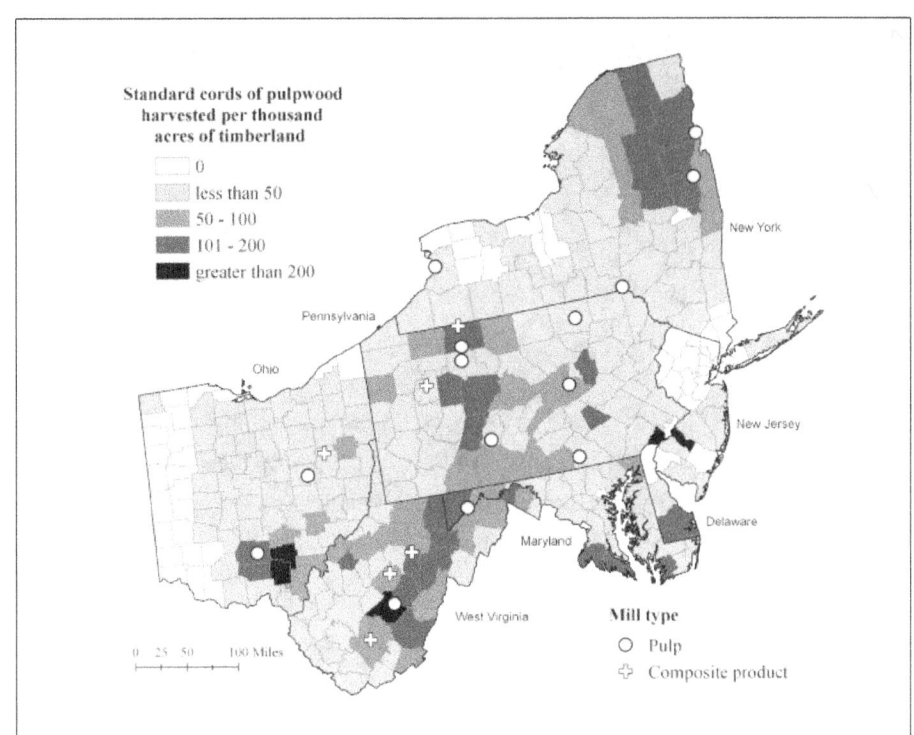

Standard cords of pulpwood harvested per thousand acres of timberland

- 0
- less than 50
- 50 - 100
- 101 - 200
- greater than 200

Mill type

- ○ Pulp
- ✣ Composite product

0 25 50 100 Miles

Figure 12.—Standard cords of pulpwood harvested per thousand acres of timberland in the Mid-Atlantic States by county, 2006. Area of timberland is based on U.S. Forest Service Inventory and Analysis data for 2006. Map shows active pulp and composite products mills. See Table 21 for pulpwood mills in the Mid-Atlantic States.

NEW ENGLAND STATES

PRODUCTION

- There were 4.1 million cords of pulpwood produced in the New England States in 2006. Eighty-five percent of the pulpwood produced came from roundwood and 15 percent came from mill residues from other primary wood processors in the New England States (Table 22).

- Soft maple and spruce, collectively, accounted for almost 30 percent of the total volume harvested for pulpwood in the New England States in 2006, with 557,000 cords and 465,000 cords, respectively. Other important species harvested for pulpwood in 2006 were aspen/balsam poplar (406,000 cords), hard maple (369,000 cords), and hemlock (313,000 cords) (Fig. 13 and Table 25).

- Eighty-four percent (3.5 million cords) of the pulpwood produced in the New England States came from Maine. New Hampshire produced 10 percent of the pulpwood, Vermont produced 5 percent, and Connecticut, Massachusetts, and Rhode Island collectively produced 1 percent (Fig. 14).

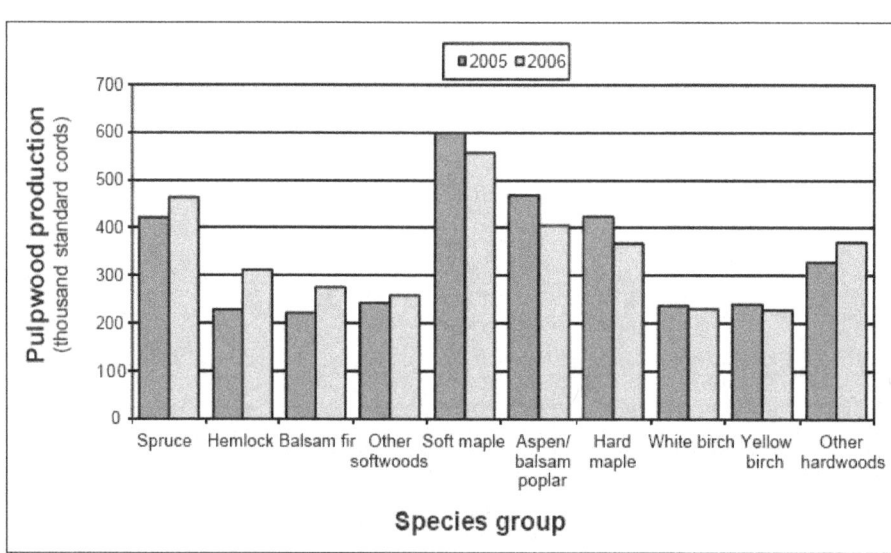

Figure 13.—Pulpwood production in the New England States by species group, 2005 and 2006.

16

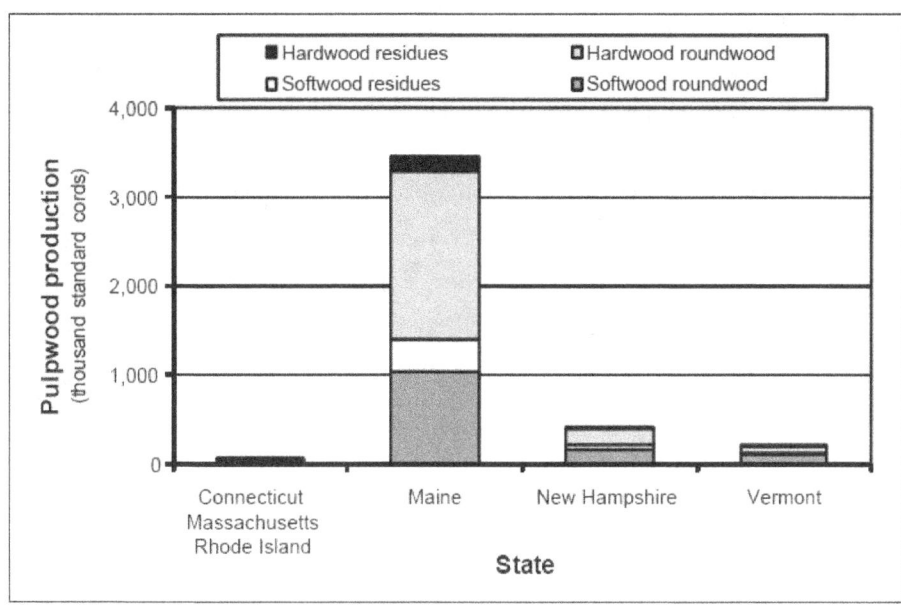

Figure 14.—Pulpwood production in the New England States by state, softwood and hardwood, and product form, 2006.

- In 2006, 96 percent (3.9 million cords) of the pulpwood produced in the New England States went to pulp mills. The remaining 166,000 cords went to composite products mills (Table 24).

- From 2005 to 2006, the production of pulpwood for pulp products decreased by 2 percent for pulp products and decreased by 15 percent for composite products (Fig. 15 and Table 25).

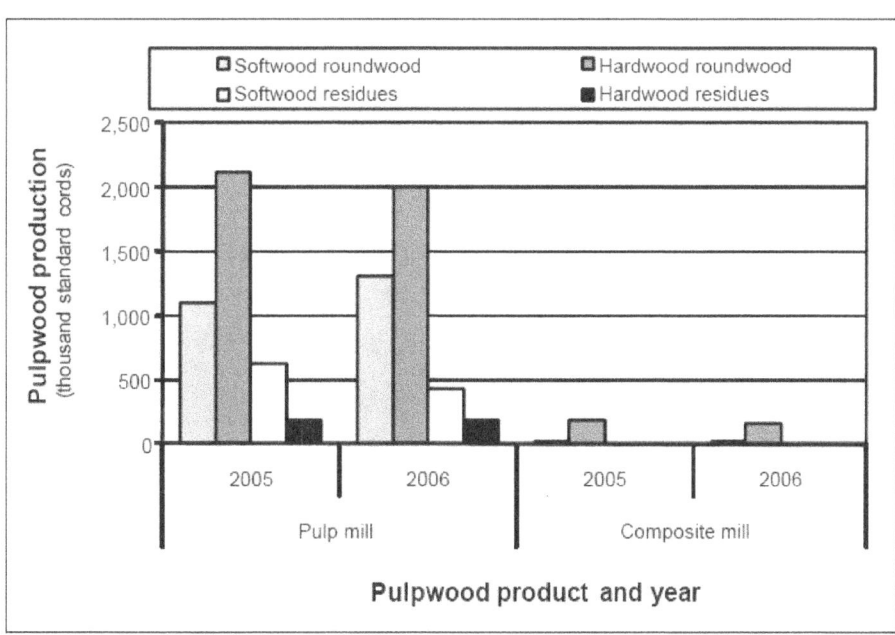

Figure 15.—Pulpwood production in the New England States by softwood and hardwood, product form, and mill type, 2006.

17

RECEIPTS

Because of the few pulpwood mills in Connecticut, Massachusetts, New Hampshire, Rhode Island, and Vermont, detailed receipt information is not reported for the New England States to avoid disclosure of information from individual mills.

- In 2006, 11 wood pulp and two composite products mills in the New England States acquired 4.4 million cords of pulpwood, a decrease of 6 percent from the year before.

- Pulp mills in Maine received 89 percent of the total volume processed by the mills in the Region.

- Eighty-three percent of the pulpwood produced in the New England States was processed by mills in the region. All but a small fraction of the wood imported for pulpwood came from Canada. Less than 1 percent of the imported pulpwood came from the Mid-Atlantic States.

INDUSTRY TRENDS AND ANALYSIS

- Pulpwood production in the New England States decreased by 3 percent from 2005 to 2006. The 1 percent increase in pulpwood production from roundwood (3.4 million cords in 2005 to 3.5 million cords in 2006) was offset by a more than 20 percent decrease in pulpwood production from mill residues (805,000 cords in 2005 to 623,000 cords in 2006).

- Roundwood harvested for pulpwood occurred in 58 of the 67 counties in the New England States (Tables 26, 27, and 28). More than half of the total harvest came from only five counties in Maine: Somerset, Aroostook, Penobscot, Oxford, and Piscataquis.

- An average of 108 cords of pulpwood was harvested per thousand acres of timberland from the 58 counties in the New England States that harvested pulpwood in 2006. Twelve counties had pulpwood harvest greater than 150 cords per thousand acres of timberland (Fig. 16).

- Three pulp mills in the New England States closed in 2005 and 2006: Groveton Paperboard, Inc., Groveton, NH, in 2005; Fraser Paper, Berlin, NH, and Georgia-Pacific, Old Town, ME, in 2006. The Georgia-Pacific mill at Old Town, ME, was purchased and re-opened by Red Shield in 2007.

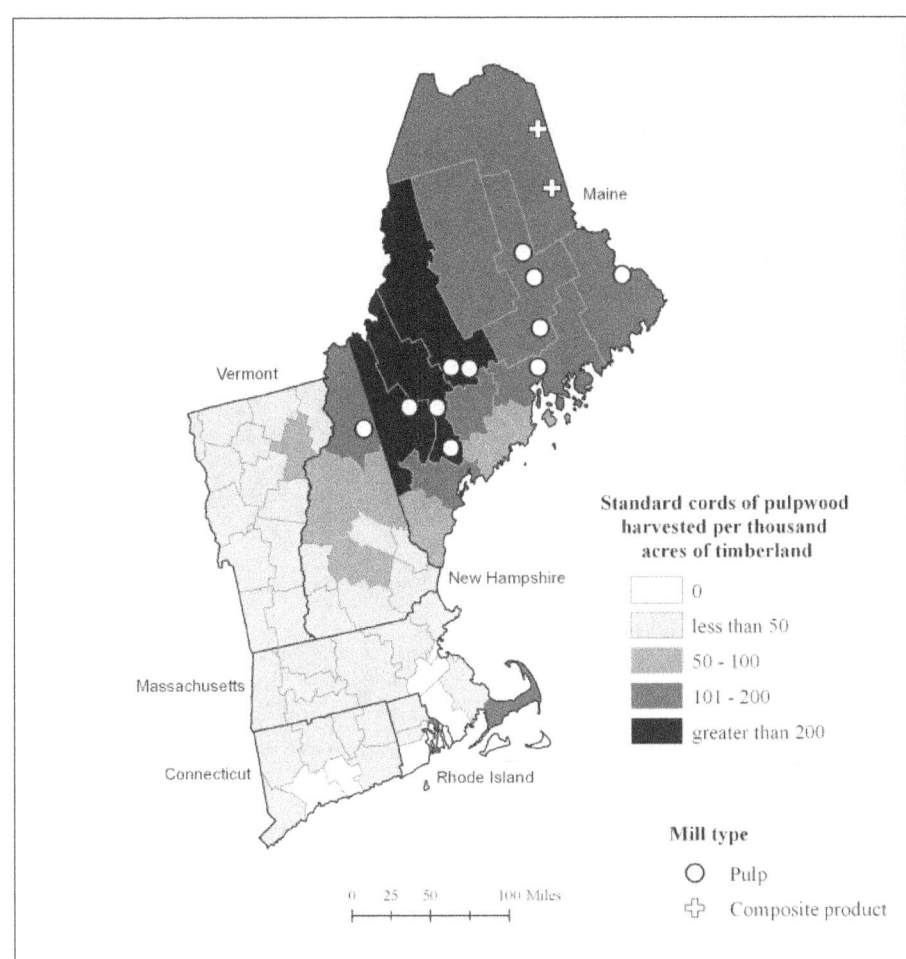

Standard cords of pulpwood harvested per thousand acres of timberland

	0
	less than 50
	50 - 100
	101 - 200
	greater than 200

Mill type

○ Pulp

✚ Composite product

0   25   50   100 Miles

Maine

Vermont

New Hampshire

Massachusetts

Connecticut

Rhode Island

Figure 16.—Standard cords of pulpwood harvested per thousand acres of timberland in the New England States by county, 2006. Area of timberland is based on U.S. Forest Service Inventory and Analysis data for 2006. Map shows active pulp and composite products mills. See Table 29 for pulpwood mills in the New England States.

- A small decrease in pulpwood production was expected in 2007 as pulp product and composite product markets continued to decline. The Fraser Paper (Berlin, NH) mill, which did run for a few months in 2006, will have no production in 2007.

PLAINS STATES

Because of few pulpwood mills in the Plains States, detailed production and receipts are not reported to avoid disclosure of information about individual mill receipts.

PRODUCTION

- In 2006, the Plains States produced 84 thousand cords of roundwood and mill residues for pulpwood production, a decrease of 26 percent from 2005 (Fig. 17).

- Residues accounted for 85 percent of the total pulpwood produced in the Plains States in 2006. Roundwood accounted for 15 percent of the total pulpwood produced, with ponderosa pine, aspen, and cottonwood being the only species harvested (Fig. 18).

- The only mill in the Plains States in 2006 was Merillat Corporation, LLC, (particleboard), in Rapid City, SD, which had an annual production capacity of 95 million square feet, ¾-inch basis.

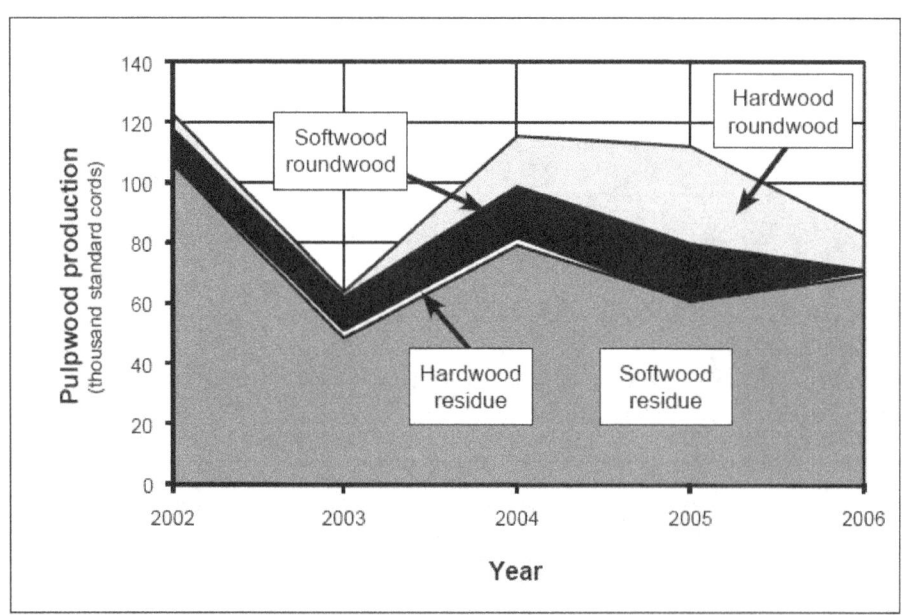

Figure 17.—Pulpwood production in the Plains States by softwood and hardwood, product form, 2002-2006.

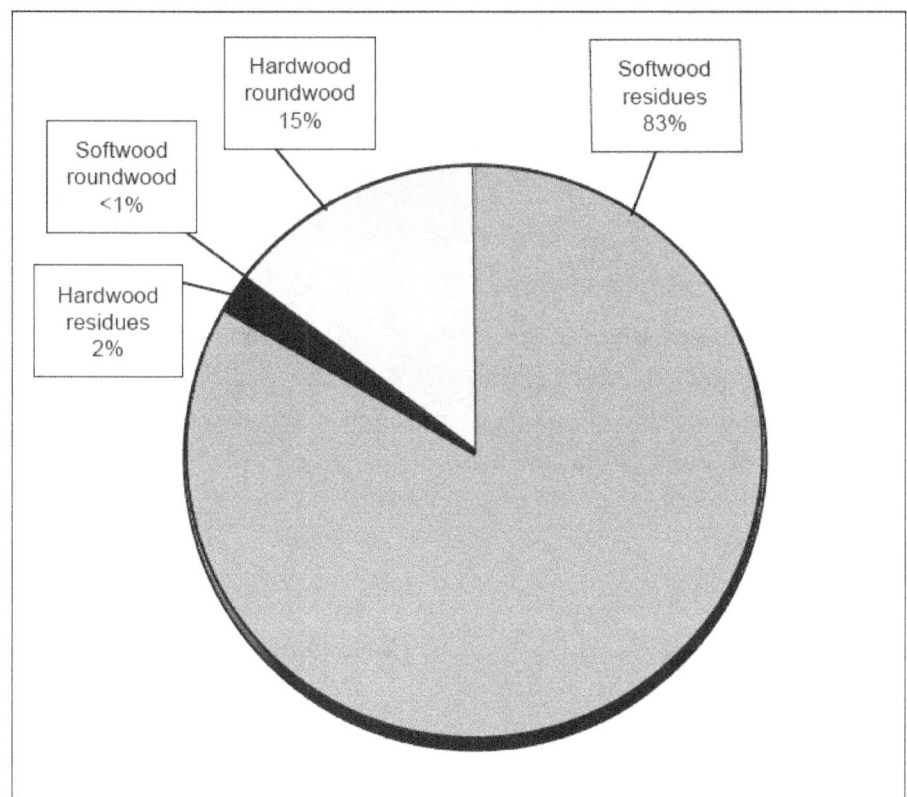

Softwood
roundwood
<1%

Hardwood
roundwood
15%

Softwood
residues
83%

Hardwood
residues
2%

Figure 18.—Pulpwood
production in the Plains
States by softwood
and hardwood, product
form, 2006.

LITERATURE CITED

Baker, Iris C.; Hansen, Bruce G.; Akers, Melody S. 2005. **Pulpwood production and consumption in the Northeast—2001.** Resour. Bull. NE-162. Newtown Square, PA: U.S. Department of Agriculture, Forest Service, Northeastern Research Station. 40 p.

APPENDIX I

DEFINITION OF TERMS

Composite products. Products manufactured from chips, wafers, strands, flakes, shavings, or sawdust and then reconstituted into a variety of panel and engineered lumber products. These products include engineered strand lumber, hardboard, medium density fiberboard, oriented strand board, and particleboard.

Consumption. The quantity of a commodity, such as pulpwood, utilized by a particular mill or group of mills. See Pulpwood receipts.

Cord. All references to cords are in standard cords. See definition of standard cord.

Exports. The volume of domestic roundwood utilized by mills outside a state or Region where timber was cut or mill residues were produced.

Forest land. Land at least 10 percent stocked by forest trees of any size, or formerly having had such tree cover, and not currently developed for nonforest use. (Note: Stocking is measured by comparing specified standards with basal area and/or number of trees, age or size, and spacing.) The minimum area for classification of forest land is 1 acre. Roadside, streamside, and shelterbelt strips of timber must have a crown width of at least 120 feet to qualify as forest land. Unimproved roads and trails, streams or other bodies of water, or clearings in forest areas shall be classed as forest if less than 120 feet wide.

Growing-stock removals. The growing-stock volume removed from the timberland inventory by harvesting roundwood products. (Note: Includes sawtimber removals, poletimber removals, and logging residues.)

Growing-stock tree. A live timberland tree of commercial species that meets specified standards of size, quality, and merchantability. (Note: Excludes rough, rotten, and dead trees.)

Growing-stock volume. Net volume of growing-stock trees 5.0 inches d.b.h. and over, from 1 foot above the ground to a minimum 4.0-inch top diameter outside bark of the central stem or to the point where the central stem breaks into limbs.

Hardwoods. Dicotyledonous trees, usually broad-leaved and deciduous.
 a) **Hard hardwoods.** Hardwood species that have wood with an average specific gravity greater than 0.50.
 b) **Soft hardwoods.** Hardwood species that have wood with an average specific gravity 0.50 or less.

Harvest residues. The total net volume of unused portions of trees cut or killed by logging. (Note: Includes both logging residues and logging slash.)

Imports. The volume of domestic roundwood or mill residues delivered to a mill or group of mills in a specific state or Region but harvested outside the state or Region.

Primary wood processor. Mill receiving roundwood or chips from roundwood for processing into products such as lumber, veneer, pulp, etc.

Primary wood processing residue. Wood materials (coarse and fine) and bark generated at manufacturing plants that process roundwood into principal products. These residues include wood products (byproducts) obtained incidental to production of principal products and wood materials not utilized for some product.
 a) **Coarse mill residue.** Wood residue suitable for chipping such as slabs, edgings, and veneer cores.
 b) **Fine mill residue.** Wood residue not suitable for chipping such as sawdust and veneer clippings.

Product form. The type of wood material used in the production of pulpwood products. See Roundwood and Primary wood processing residue.

Pulpwood. Roundwood (includes roundwood that is chipped) and primary wood processing residues that will be reduced to individual wood fibers, fiber bundles, chips, or particles by chemical or mechanical means used to make a broad generic group of products that include pulp and composite products.

Pulpwood production. The volume of roundwood harvested, plus the wood residue volume produced by sawmills, veneer mills, etc. within a state or region and used for pulp, particleboard, waferboard, oriented strandboard, medium density fiberboard, or engineered lumber, regardless of where it is consumed.

Pulpwood receipts. The quantity or volume of roundwood and primary wood processing residues received at a mill or by a group of mills in a state or region, regardless of geographic source. Volume of roundwood receipts is equal to the volume of roundwood retained in a state or region plus roundwood imported from other states or regions.

Residue. See Primary wood processing residue.

Retained. Roundwood and primary wood processing residue volume harvested from and processed by mills within the same state or region.

Roundwood. Any primary use of a tree (includes trees harvested and chipped) for use as industrial products such as saw logs, pulpwood, or veneer logs, intended to be processed into primary wood products such as lumber, wood pulp, or sheathing, at primary wood processor.

Roundwood production. The total volume of known roundwood harvested within a state or region, regardless of where it is consumed. Roundwood production is the sum of timber harvested and used within a state or region and all roundwood exported to other states or Regions.

Softwoods. Coniferous trees, usually evergreen, having needles or scale-like leaves.

Standard cord. A unit of measure applied to roundwood, usually bolts or split wood. It is a stack of wood 4 feet high, 4 feet wide, and 8 feet long encompassing 128 cubic feet of wood, bark, and air space. The Northern Region estimates 79 cubic feet of wood per cord for pulpwood in the Central States, Lake States, and Plains States, and 85 cubic feet of wood per cord for pulpwood in the Mid-Atlantic States and New England States.

Timber product output. The volume of roundwood products produced from an area's forests plus the volume of byproduct recovered from mill residues.

Timberland. Forest land that is producing, or is capable of producing, in excess of 20 cubic feet per acre per year of roundwood products under natural conditions, is not withdrawn from timber utilization by statute or administrative regulation, and is not associated with urban or rural development.

Tree. A woody plant usually having one or more perennial stems, a more or less definitely formed crown of foliage, and a height of at least 12 feet at maturity.

APPENDIX II

COMMON AND SCIENTIFIC NAMES OF TREE SPECIES WITHIN SPECIES GROUPS MENTIONED IN THIS REPORT

SOFTWOODS

Cedars
    Atlantic white-cedar   *Chamaecyparis thyoides*
    Rocky Mountain juniper   *Juniperus scopulorum*
    Eastern redcedar   *Juniperus virginiana*
    Northern white-cedar   *Thuja occidentalis*

Balsam fir   *Abies balsamea*

Eastern hemlock   *Tsuga canadensis*

Tamarack   *Larix laricina*

Jack pine   *Pinus banksiana*

Shortleaf pine   *Pinus echinata*

Loblolly pine   *Pinus taeda*

Ponderosa pine   *Pinus ponderosa*

Red pine   *Pinus resinosa*

White pine   *Pinus strobus*

Other pines
    Table Mountain pine   *Pinus pungens*
    Pitch pine   *Pinus rigida*
    Pond pine   *Pinus serotina*
    Scotch pine   *Pinus sylvestris*
    Virginia pine   *Pinus virginiana*
    Austrian pine   *Pinus nigra*

Spruce
    Norway spruce   *Picea abies*
    White spruce   *Picea glauca*
    Black spruce   *Picea mariana*
    Blue spruce   *Picea pungens*
    Red spruce   *Picea rubens*

HARDWOODS

Ash
    White ash   *Fraxinus americana*
    Black ash   *Fraxinus nigra*
    Green ash   *Fraxinus pennsylvanica*
    Pumpkin ash   *Fraxinus profunda*
    Blue ash   *Fraxinus quadrangulata*

Aspen/balsam poplar
 Balsam poplar   *Populus balsamifera*
 Bigtooth aspen   *Populus grandidentata*
 Quaking aspen   *Populus tremuloides*
Basswood
 American basswood *Tilia americana*
 White basswood   *Tilia americana* var. *heterophylla*
American beech   *Fagus grandifolia*
Yellow birch   *Betula alleghaniensis*
White birch   *Betula papyrifera*
Other birches
 Sweet birch   *Betula lenta*
 River birch   *Betula nigra*
 Gray birch   *Betula populifolia*
Black cherry   *Prunus serotina*
Black walnut   *Juglans nigra*
Cottonwood
 Eastern cottonwood *Populus deltoides*
 Swamp cottonwood *Populus heterophylla*
Elm
 Winged elm   *Ulmus alata*
 American elm   *Ulmus americana*
 Siberian elm   *Ulmus pumila*
 Slippery elm   *Ulmus rubra*
 Rock elm   *Ulmus thomasii*
Hickory
 Mockernut hickory   *Carya alba*
 Water hickory   *Carya aquatica*
 Bitternut hickory   *Carya cordiformis*
 Pignut hickory   *Carya glabra*
 Pecan   *Carya illinoinensis*
 Shellbark hickory   *Carya laciniosa*
 Shagbark hickory   *Carya ovata*
 Black hickory   *Carya texana*
Hard maples
 Black maple   *Acer nigrum*
 Norway maple   *Acer platanoides*
 Sugar maple   *Acer saccharum*
Soft maples
 Boxelder   *Acer negundo*
 Red maple   *Acer rubrum*
 Silver maple   *Acer saccharinum*
Red oak group
 Scarlet oak   *Quercus coccinea*
 Northern pin oak   *Quercus ellipsoidalis*
 Southern red oak   *Quercus falcata*
 Shingle oak   *Quercus imbricaria*
 Blackjack oak   *Quercus marilandica*
 Water oak   *Quercus nigra*
 Cherrybark oak   *Quercus pagoda*

Pin oak	*Quercus palustris*
Willow oak	*Quercus phellos*
Northern red oak	*Quercus rubra*
Shumard oak	*Quercus shumardii*
Black oak	*Quercus velutina*
White oak group	
White oak	*Quercus alba*
Swamp white oak	*Quercus bicolor*
Overcup oak	*Quercus lyrata*
Bur oak	*Quercus macrocarpa*
Swamp chestnut oak	*Quercus michauxii*
Chinkapin oak	*Quercus muehlenbergii*
Chestnut oak	*Quercus prinus*
Post oak	*Quercus stellata*
Sweetgum	*Liquidambar styraciflua*
American sycamore	*Platanus occidentalis*
Tupelo/gum	
Water tupelo	*Nyssa aquatica*
Swamp tupelo	*Nyssa biflora*
Blackgum	*Nyssa sylvatica*
Yellow-poplar	*Liriodendron tulipifera*
Other hardwoods	
Ohio buckeye	*Aesculus glabra*
Northern catalpa	*Catalpa speciosa*
Sugarberry	*Celtis laevigata*
Hackberry	*Celtis occidentalis*
Flowering dogwood	*Cornus florida*
Common persimmon	*Diospyros virginiana*
Waterlocust	*Gleditsia aquatica*
Honeylocust	*Gleditsia triacanthos*
Kentucky coffeetree	*Gymnocladus dioicus*
American holly	*Ilex opaca*
Butternut	*Juglans cinerea*
Cucumbertree	*Magnolia acuminata*
White mulberry	*Morus alba*
Red mulberry	*Morus rubra*
Paulownia or empress-tree	*Paulownia tomentosa*
Pin cherry	*Prunus pensylvanica*
Chokecherry	*Prunus virginiana*
Black locust	*Robinia pseudoacacia*
White willow	*Salix alba*
Black willow	*Salix nigra*
Weeping willow	*Salix sepulcralis*
Sassafras	*Sassafras albidum*

APPENDIX III

CONVERSION FACTORS USED IN THE NORTHERN REGION

Standard cords of roundwood per green ton:
(green tons x factor = standard cords)

Species	Factor	Species	Factor
Softwoods	0.4688	White birch	0.4018
Northern white-cedar	.6329	Yellow birch	.3723
Balsam fir	.4688	River birch	.3871
Hemlock	.4150	Sweetgum	.3669
Jack pine	.4688	Yellow-poplar	.4219
Red pine	.4688	Blackgum	.3779
White pine	.4777	Sycamore	.4083
Shortleaf pine	.3956	Cottonwood	.4291
Spruce	.5014	Elm	.4018
Tamarack	.4291	Hickory	.3701
Hardwoods	.3939	Hard maple	.3617
Soft hardwoods	.4171	Soft maple	.4083
Hard hardwoods	.3708	Black cherry	.4688
Ash	.4330	Red oak	.3444
Aspen	.4291	White oak	.3723
Balsam poplar	.4083	Black oak	.3444
Basswood	.5167	Other hardwoods	.4777
Beech	.3956		

LIST OF TABLES

TABLES

Table 1.—Production and imports of pulpwood in standard cords, unpeeled, Central States, 2006

Product form, species group, and destination	Production by state[a]					Imports	Total receipts
	Illinois	Indiana	Iowa	Missouri	Regional Total	Lake States	
Roundwood							
Softwood							
Mid-Atlantic States	32	3,510	--	--	3,542	--	--
Southern States	2,113	--	--	29	2,142	--	--
Total	2,145	3,510	--	29	5,684	--	--
Soft hardwood							
Central States	1,193	6,067	--	878	8,138	--	8,138
Lake States	10	--	--	--	10	--	--
Mid-Atlantic States	--	11	--	--	11	--	--
Southern States	3,323	2,879	--	3,332	9,534	--	--
Total	4,526	8,957	--	4,209	17,692	--	8,138
Hard hardwood							
Central States	1,737	8,828	--	463	11,028	--	11,028
Lake States	0	--	--	--	0	--	--
Mid-Atlantic States	--	23	--	--	23	--	--
Southern States	6,047	5,134	--	32,825	44,006	--	--
Total	7,784	13,985	--	33,288	55,057	--	11,028
Total all roundwood							
Central States	2,930	14,895	--	1,341	19,166	--	19,166
Lake States	10	--	--	--	10	--	--
Mid-Atlantic States	32	3,544	--	--	3,575	--	--
Southern States	11,483	8,013	--	36,186	55,682	--	--
Total	14,454	26,452	--	37,527	78,433	--	19,166
Residues							
Softwood							
Central States	--	--	6,400	--	6,400	14,400	20,800
Mid-Atlantic States	--	480	--	--	480	--	--
Southern States	--	--	--	491	491	--	--
Total	--	480	6,400	491	7,371	14,400	20,800

Hardwood

Central States	--	38,147	298	5,665	44,110	3,200	47,310
Lake States	--	--	6,073	--	6,073	--	--
Mid-Atlantic States	--	10,310	--	--	10,310	--	--
Southern States	10,809	77,987	--	162,820	251,616	--	--
Total	10,809	126,444	6,371	168,485	312,110	3,200	47,310
Total all residues							
Central States	--	38,147	6,698	5,665	50,510	17,600	68,110
Lake States	--	--	6,073	--	6,073	--	--
Mid-Atlantic States	--	10,790	--	--	10,790	--	--
Southern States	10,809	77,987	--	163,311	252,107	--	--
Total	10,809	126,924	12,771	168,977	319,481	17,600	68,110
Total all wood material							
Central States	2,930	53,042	6,698	7,006	69,676	17,600	87,276
Lake States	10	--	6,073	--	6,083	--	--
Mid-Atlantic States	32	14,334	--	--	14,366	--	--
Southern States	22,292	86,000	--	199,497	307,789	--	--
Total	25,264	153,376	12,771	206,504	397,914	17,600	87,276

[a] Vertical columns of figures under the box heading "Production by State" present the amount of roundwood cut or residue generated in each state

All table cells without observations are indicated by -- . Table value of 0 indicates the volume rounds to less than 1 standard cord, unpeeled. Columns and rows may not add to their totals due to rounding.

Table 2.—Central States pulpwood production in standard cords, unpeeled, by product form and species group, 2002-2006

Product form and species group	Year				
	2002	2003	2004	2005	2006
Roundwood					
Softwoods	3,432	5,485	3,854	6,064	5,684
Soft hardwoods	25,783	31,393	30,365	23,961	17,692
Hard hardwoods	121,600	113,501	131,933	104,581	55,057
Total	150,815	150,380	166,151	134,606	78,433
Residues					
Softwood	1,860	1,860	1,071	39,713	7,371
Hardwood	274,219	310,161	316,767	298,216	312,110
Total	276,079	312,021	317,838	337,929	319,481
Total all wood material	426,895	462,400	483,989	472,535	397,914

Columns may not add to their totals due to rounding.

Table 3.—Average production of active wood-pulp by company, location,
and type of pulp produced, Central States, 2006

Product and company	Location	Product produced	Average production
Pulp mills			
International Paper Co.	Terre Haute, Indiana	Groundwood/mechanical pulp	100 tons of pulp per day
Jeld-Wen Wood Fiber Division	Dubuque, Iowa	Medium density fiberboard	80 tons of pulp per day
Huebert Fiberboard, Inc.	Boonville, Missouri	Groundwood/mechanical pulp	80 tons of pulp per day

Table 4.—Production and imports of pulpwood in standard cords, unpeeled, Lake States, 2006

Product form, species group, and destination	Production by state[a]				Imports				Total receipts
	Michigan	Minnesota	Wisconsin	Regional Total	Central States	Plains States	Canada	Total imports	
Softwood roundwood									
Northern white-cedar									
Michigan	1,290	--	30	1,320	--	--	1	1	1,321
Total	1,290	--	30	1,320	--	--	1	1	1,321
Balsam fir									
Canada	9,116	1,645	--	10,761	--	--	--	--	--
Michigan	44,985	--	4,048	49,033	--	--	39	39	49,072
Minnesota	623	158,796	23,527	182,946	--	--	97	97	183,044
Wisconsin	3,431	--	41,470	44,901	--	--	--	--	44,901
Total	58,154	160,441	69,046	287,641	--	--	137	137	277,017
Hemlock									
Michigan	53,435	--	1,908	55,343	--	--	18	18	55,361
Wisconsin	1,761	--	16,055	17,816	--	--	--	--	17,816
Total	55,196	--	17,963	73,159	--	--	18	18	73,177
Jack pine									
Canada	1,740	--	--	1,740	--	--	--	--	--
Michigan	73,622	--	6,118	79,740	--	--	20	20	79,760
Minnesota	18	115,389	9,198	124,606	--	8	782	791	125,397
Wisconsin	4,079	--	64,660	68,739	--	--	--	--	68,739
Total	79,460	115,389	79,976	274,826	--	8	802	810	273,896
Red pine									
Canada	1,471	--	--	1,471	--	--	--	--	--
Michigan	42,819	--	3,213	46,032	--	--	55	55	46,087
Minnesota	8	29,089	4,144	33,241	--	--	12	12	33,252
Wisconsin	1,064	462	148,282	149,809	--	--	--	--	149,809
Total	45,362	29,551	155,639	230,552	--	--	67	67	229,148
White pine									
Canada	1,787	--	--	1,787	--	--	--	--	--
Michigan	5,223	--	272	5,494	--	--	5	5	5,500
Minnesota	0	1,155	262	1,417	--	--	--	--	1,417
Wisconsin	537	134	57,041	57,712	--	--	--	--	57,712
Total	7,547	1,289	57,574	66,410	--	--	5	5	64,628
Other pines									
Minnesota	--	838	--	838	--	--	--	--	838
Wisconsin	--	--	21	21	--	--	--	--	21
Total	--	838	21	859	--	--	--	--	859

Spruce								
Canada	12,285	1,939	--	14,224	--	--	--	--
Michigan	15,221	954	--	16,175	--	1,235	1,235	17,410
Minnesota	32	169,856	4,738	174,626	--	3,262	3,262	177,887
Wisconsin	21,593	22,890	84,634	129,117	--	2,600	2,600	131,717
Total	49,130	194,685	90,326	334,142	--	7,097	7,097	327,015
Tamarack								
Canada	--	2,085	--	2,085	--	--	--	--
Michigan	11,129	--	2,513	13,641	--	6	6	13,647
Minnesota	--	31,749	45	31,794	--	14	14	31,808
Wisconsin	766	--	10,447	11,213	--	--	--	11,213
Total	11,894	33,834	13,005	58,733	--	20	20	56,668
Total softwood roundwood								
Canada	26,399	5,669	--	32,068	--	--	--	--
Michigan	247,724	--	19,056	266,780	--	1,380	1,380	268,159
Minnesota	681	506,872	41,914	549,467	8	4,167	4,176	553,643
Wisconsin	33,230	23,486	422,610	479,327	--	2,600	2,600	481,927
Total	308,034	536,027	483,581	1,327,642	8	8,147	8,156	1,303,730
Softwood residues								
Canada	22,828	21,547	--	44,375	--	--	--	--
Michigan	182,253	--	1,088	183,341	--	--	--	183,341
Minnesota	--	99,534	1,669	101,203	--	--	--	101,203
Other[b]	--	2,400	12,000	14,400	--	--	--	14,400
Wisconsin	79,328	--	79,302	158,631	--	6,765	6,765	165,396
Total	284,410	123,481	94,059	501,950	--	6,765	6,765	449,940
Total softwood material								
Canada	49,227	27,216	--	76,443	--	--	--	--
Michigan	429,977	--	20,144	450,121	--	1,380	1,380	451,501
Minnesota	681	606,406	43,583	650,671	8	4,167	4,176	654,846
Other[b]	--	2,400	12,000	14,400	--	--	--	--
Wisconsin	112,559	23,486	501,913	637,958	--	9,365	9,365	647,323
Total	592,444	659,509	577,640	1,829,592	8	14,913	14,921	1,753,670

(Table 4 continued on next page)

(Table 4 continued)

Product form, species group, and destination	Production by state[a]				Imports				Total receipts
	Michigan	Minnesota	Wisconsin	Regional Total	Central States	Plains States	Canada	Total imports	
Hardwood roundwood									
Ash									
Michigan	21,300	--	4,173	25,473	--	--	1,276	1,276	26,749
Minnesota	1,635	15,003	7,242	23,880	--	--	1,561	1,561	25,441
Wisconsin	1,170	1	30,972	32,143	0	--	0	0	32,143
Total	24,105	15,004	42,387	81,496	0	--	2,837	2,838	84,334
Aspen/balsam poplar									
Canada	3,862	--	--	3,862	--	--	--	--	--
Michigan	518,215	--	5,990	524,204	--	--	22,537	22,537	546,742
Minnesota	4,651	1,575,327	117,683	1,697,661	--	11,963	126,427	138,390	1,836,052
Wisconsin	32,427	23,913	691,155	747,495	--	--	18,288	18,288	765,784
Total	559,155	1,599,240	814,827	2,973,223	--	11,963	167,253	179,216	3,148,577
Basswood									
Michigan	45,701	--	11,734	57,436	--	--	780	780	58,215
Minnesota	--	11,995	6,995	18,990	--	--	--	--	18,990
Wisconsin	225	508	28,981	29,713	--	--	--	--	29,713
Total	45,926	12,503	47,710	106,139	--	--	780	780	106,919
Beech									
Michigan	86,618	--	9,907	96,525	--	--	3,932	3,932	100,457
Minnesota	121	--	--	121	--	--	--	--	121
Wisconsin	4,278	--	2,536	6,814	--	--	--	--	6,814
Total	91,016	--	12,443	103,459	--	--	3,932	3,932	107,391
White birch									
Michigan	57,354	--	10,863	68,217	--	--	3,690	3,690	71,907
Minnesota	740	161,318	26,464	188,522	--	--	839	839	189,361
Wisconsin	1,264	2	13,403	14,668	--	--	--	--	14,668
Total	59,357	161,320	50,730	271,407	--	--	4,529	4,529	275,936
Yellow birch									
Michigan	27,472	--	6,868	34,340	--	--	2,242	2,242	36,582
Wisconsin	822	--	7,350	8,173	--	--	--	--	8,173
Total	28,294	--	14,218	42,513	--	--	2,242	2,242	44,755
Cottonwood									
Minnesota	--	3	--	3	--	270	--	270	272
Wisconsin	47	5	481	533	--	--	--	--	533
Total	47	8	481	535	--	270	--	270	805
Elm									
Michigan	32	--	--	32	--	--	0	0	32
Wisconsin	318	5	3,523	3,846	--	--	--	--	3,846
Total	350	5	3,523	3,878	--	--	0	0	3,878
Hickory									
Wisconsin	100	--	673	773	--	--	--	--	773
Total	100	--	673	773	--	--	--	--	773

Hard maple								
Michigan	353,151	--	67,739	420,890	--	--	22,477	443,367
Minnesota	9,763	31,363	44,983	86,109	--	--	76	86,185
Wisconsin	16,361	30	126,862	143,252	--	--	--	143,252
Total	379,274	31,393	239,584	650,251	--	--	22,553	672,804
Soft maple								
Michigan	331,990	--	61,924	393,914	--	--	22,082	415,995
Minnesota	33,063	85,990	140,242	259,295	--	--	257	259,552
Wisconsin	13,960	167	98,195	112,322	10	--	10	112,332
Total	379,013	86,157	300,361	765,531	10	--	22,348	787,879
Red oak								
Michigan	28,174	--	3,509	31,683	--	--	1,010	32,693
Minnesota	--	133	357	490	--	--	--	490
Wisconsin	379	8	121,656	122,043	--	--	--	122,043
Total	28,554	142	125,521	154,216	--	--	1,010	155,227
White oak								
Michigan	3,123	--	--	3,123	--	--	--	3,123
Minnesota	--	54	--	54	--	--	--	54
Wisconsin	42	4	16,572	16,618	--	--	--	16,618
Total	3,165	58	16,572	19,795	--	--	--	19,795
Other hardwoods								
Michigan	155,976	--	59,793	215,769	--	--	2,208	217,977
Wisconsin	--	0	72	72	--	--	--	72
Total	155,976	0	59,865	215,841	--	--	2,208	218,049
Total hardwood roundwood								
Canada	3,862	--	--	3,862	--	--	--	--
Michigan	1,629,106	--	242,500	1,871,606	--	--	82,235	1,953,840
Minnesota	49,972	1,881,187	343,966	2,275,125	12,233	--	141,393	2,416,518
Wisconsin	71,394	24,643	1,142,429	1,238,466	10	--	18,299	1,256,764
Total	1,754,333	1,905,830	1,728,895	5,389,058	12,233	--	241,926	5,627,122
Hardwood residues								
Canada	11,308	--	11,308	11,308	--	--	--	--
Michigan	123,822	--	14,146	137,968	--	--	--	137,968
Minnesota	--	95,630	2,326	97,955	--	--	7,302	105,257
Other[b]	--	--	3,200	3,200	3,200	--	--	--
Wisconsin	5,125	5,900	204,683	215,708	6,073	6,073	6,073	221,781
Total	140,255	101,530	224,355	466,140	6,083	6,073	13,374	465,006
Total hardwood material								
Canada	15,170	--	15,170	15,170	--	--	--	--
Michigan	1,752,928	--	256,646	2,009,574	--	--	82,235	2,091,809
Minnesota	49,972	1,976,816	346,292	2,373,080	12,233	12,233	148,694	2,521,775
Other[b]	--	--	3,200	3,200	12,233	--	--	--
Wisconsin	76,519	30,543	1,347,112	1,454,174	6,083	--	24,372	1,478,546
Total	1,894,588	2,007,360	1,953,250	5,855,198	12,233	12,233	255,300	6,092,129

(Table 4 continued on next page)

(Table 4 continued)

Product form, species group, and destination	Production by state[a]				Imports				Total receipts
	Michigan	Minnesota	Wisconsin	Regional Total	Central States	Plains States	Canada	Total imports	
Total all roundwood									
Canada	30,260	5,669	--	35,929	--	--	--	--	--
Michigan	1,876,830	--	261,556	2,138,386	--	--	83,614	83,614	2,222,000
Minnesota	50,654	2,388,058	385,880	2,824,592	--	12,241	133,327	145,569	2,970,161
Wisconsin	104,624	48,130	1,565,039	1,717,793	10	--	20,889	20,899	1,738,691
Total	2,062,367	2,441,857	2,212,475	6,716,700	10	12,241	237,830	250,082	6,930,852
Total all residues									
Canada	34,136	21,547	--	55,684	--	--	--	--	--
Michigan	306,075	--	15,234	321,309	--	--	--	--	321,309
Minnesota	--	195,164	3,995	199,159	--	--	7,302	7,302	206,460
Other[b]	--	2,400	15,200	17,600	--	--	--	--	--
Wisconsin	84,453	5,900	283,986	374,339	6,073	--	6,765	12,838	387,177
Total	424,665	225,011	318,415	968,090	6,073	--	14,067	20,140	914,946
Total all wood material									
Canada	64,397	27,216	--	91,613	--	--	--	--	--
Michigan	2,182,905	--	276,790	2,459,695	--	--	83,614	83,614	2,543,309
Minnesota	50,654	2,583,222	389,875	3,023,751	--	12,241	140,629	152,870	3,176,621
Other[b]	--	2,400	15,200	17,600	--	--	--	--	--
Wisconsin	189,077	54,030	1,849,025	2,092,132	6,083	--	27,654	33,737	2,125,869
Total	2,487,032	2,666,868	2,530,890	7,684,790	6,083	12,241	251,897	270,221	7,845,799

[a] Vertical columns of figures under the box heading "Production by State" present the amount of roundwood cut or residue generated in each state
[b] Pulpwood shipped to mills outside of region.
All table cells without observations are indicated by --. Table value of 0 indicates the volume rounds to less than 1 standard cord, unpeeled. Columns and rows may not add to their totals due to rounding.

Table 5.—Lake States pulpwood production in thousand standard cords, unpeeled, from roundwood by state and species group, 2002-2006

All species

State	2002	2003	2004	2005	2006
Michigan	2,451	2,497	2,658	2,550	2,062
Minnesota	2,907	2,830	2,876	3,020	2,442
Wisconsin	3,087	3,174	3,302	3,311	2,212
Total Lake States	8,446	8,501	8,836	8,881	6,717

Pine

State	2002	2003	2004	2005	2006
Michigan	192	198	264	285	132
Minnesota	163	128	205	200	147
Wisconsin	521	524	445	500	293
Total Lake States	875	850	914	985	573

Spruce

State	2002	2003	2004	2005	2006
Michigan	47	49	74	64	49
Minnesota	215	218	165	184	195
Wisconsin	49	65	58	63	90
Total Lake States	311	332	297	311	334

Balsam fir

State	2002	2003	2004	2005	2006
Michigan	70	66	79	65	58
Minnesota	169	168	167	191	160
Wisconsin	71	71	78	101	69
Total Lake States	311	306	324	357	288

Other softwoods

State	2002	2003	2004	2005	2006
Michigan	84	91	87	72	68
Minnesota	28	59	40	62	34
Wisconsin	40	46	46	51	31
Total Lake States	152	196	173	185	133

Aspen/balsam poplar

State	2002	2003	2004	2005	2006
Michigan	866	906	894	868	559
Minnesota	2,067	1,915	1,914	1,923	1,599
Wisconsin	1,001	991	984	943	815
Total Lake States	3,934	3,812	3,791	3,734	2,973

Birch

State	2002	2003	2004	2005	2006
Michigan	144	144	148	123	88
Minnesota	166	219	240	258	161
Wisconsin	251	264	316	316	65
Total Lake States	561	626	704	697	314

Maple

State	2002	2003	2004	2005	2006
Michigan	810	794	837	826	758
Minnesota	72	93	99	107	118
Wisconsin	793	826	884	910	540
Total Lake States	1,675	1,713	1,820	1,843	1,416

Other hardwoods

State	2002	2003	2004	2005	2006
Michigan	238	248	275	248	349
Minnesota	27	30	47	94	28
Wisconsin	362	388	492	427	309
Total Lake States	627	666	813	769	686

Table columns may not add due to rounding.

43

Table 6.—**Pulpwood production in standard cords, unpeeled, by mill type, product form, state of origin, and species group, Lake States, 2006**

Product form and species group	State of origin for pulp mills				State of origin for composite mills			
	All States	Michigan	Minnesota	Wisconsin	All States	Michigan	Minnesota	Wisconsin
Softwood roundwood								
Northern white-cedar	1,320	1,290	--	30	--	--	--	--
Balsam fir	266,304	50,507	153,461	62,336	21,337	7,647	6,980	6,710
Hemlock	73,159	55,196	--	17,963	--	--	--	--
Jack pine	166,457	49,158	44,410	72,890	108,368	30,302	70,979	7,087
Red pine	189,969	29,689	10,244	150,036	40,584	15,673	19,307	5,604
White pine	63,277	7,166	501	55,610	3,133	381	788	1,964
Other pine	21	--	--	21	838	--	838	--
Spruce	329,614	47,602	192,667	89,345	4,528	1,528	2,018	981
Tamarack	35,182	6,161	18,623	10,398	23,552	5,734	15,212	2,606
Total softwood roundwood	1,125,303	246,769	419,906	458,628	202,339	61,265	116,121	24,953
Hardwood roundwood								
Ash	70,882	21,427	7,849	41,606	10,614	2,678	7,155	780
Aspen/balsam poplar	1,389,113	234,162	716,525	438,426	1,584,109	324,993	882,716	376,401
Basswood	40,364	16,250	4,187	19,927	65,775	29,676	8,316	27,783
Beech	100,937	88,494	--	12,443	2,523	2,523	--	--
White birch	180,012	51,337	84,381	44,294	91,395	8,020	76,939	6,436
Yellow birch	42,430	28,229	83	14,201	83	66	--	18
Cottonwood	533	47	5	481	3	--	--	3
Elm	3,878	350	5	3,523	3	--	3	--
Hickory	773	100	--	673	--	--	--	--
Hard maple	592,066	341,605	16,549	233,912	58,185	37,669	14,844	5,672
Soft maple	640,910	291,108	55,229	294,573	124,621	87,905	30,928	5,788
Red oak group	154,112	28,449	142	125,521	104	104	--	--
White oak group	19,795	3,165	58	16,572	--	--	--	--
Other hardwoods	20,582	16,581	0	4,001	195,259	139,395	--	55,864
Total hardwood roundwood	3,256,386	1,121,304	884,929	1,250,153	2,132,672	633,029	1,020,900	478,742
Total Roundwood	4,381,689	1,368,073	1,304,835	1,708,781	2,335,011	694,294	1,137,021	503,695
Residues								
Softwood	459,104	261,582	121,018	76,505	42,846	22,828	2,463	17,555
Hardwood	380,452	125,745	94,613	160,094	85,688	14,510	6,917	64,261
Total residues	839,556	387,327	215,631	236,599	128,534	37,338	9,380	81,816
State total	5,221,245	1,755,399	1,520,466	1,945,379	2,463,545	731,633	1,146,402	585,511

All table cells without observations are indicated by -- . Table value of 0 indicates the volume rounds to less than 1 standard cord, unpeeled. Columns and rows may not add to their totals due to rounding.

Table 7.—Pulpwood production in standard cords, unpeeled, by mill type, product form, species group, and percent change, Lake States, 2005 and 2006

Product form and species group	Pulp mills			Composite mills		
	2005	2006	Percent change	2005	2006	Percent change
Softwood roundwood						
Northern white-cedar	2,294	1,320	-42%	371	--	--
Balsam fir	331,813	266,304	-20%	24,891	21,337	-14%
Hemlock	92,130	73,159	-21%	--	--	--
Jack pine	287,570	166,457	-42%	255,022	108,368	-58%
Red pine	309,097	189,969	-39%	55,059	40,584	-26%
White pine	66,740	63,277	-5%	5,943	3,133	-47%
Other pine	--	21	--	5,639	838	-85%
Spruce	305,079	329,614	8%	5,758	4,528	-21%
Tamarack	67,776	35,182	-48%	22,473	23,552	5%
Other softwoods	--	--	--	90	--	--
Total softwood roundwood	1,462,499	1,125,303	-23%	375,245	202,339	-46%
Hardwood roundwood						
Ash	166,982	70,882	-58%	18,370	10,614	-42%
Aspen/balsam poplar	1,561,562	1,389,113	-11%	2,172,754	1,584,109	-27%
Basswood	103,620	40,364	-61%	66,088	65,775	0%
Beech	59,361	100,937	70%	3,876	2,523	-35%
White birch	499,323	180,012	-64%	134,183	91,395	-32%
Yellow birch	62,907	42,430	-33%	224	83	-63%
Cottonwood	589	533	-10%	367	3	-99%
Elm	28,588	3,878	-86%	143	--	--
Hickory	3,725	773	-79%	--	--	--
Hard maple	858,118	592,066	-31%	57,616	58,185	1%
Soft maple	773,473	640,910	-17%	153,787	124,621	-19%
Red oak group	222,035	154,112	-31%	4,620	104	-98%
White oak group	60,185	19,795	-67%	71	--	--
Other hardwoods	25,898	20,582	-21%	4,577	195,259	4166%
Total hardwood roundwood	4,426,367	3,256,386	-26%	2,616,677	2,132,672	-18%
Total Roundwood	5,888,866	4,381,689	-26%	2,991,922	2,335,011	-22%
Residues						
Softwood	382,416	459,104	20%	93,254	42,846	-54%
Hardwood	351,248	380,452	8%	107,943	85,688	-21%
Total residues	733,665	839,556	14%	201,197	128,534	-36%
State total	6,622,531	5,221,248	-21%	3,193,119	2,463,545	-23%

All table cells without observations are indicated by -- . Table value of 0 indicates the volume rounds to less than 1 standard cord, unpeeled. Columns and rows may not add to their totals due to rounding.

Table 8.—Pulpwood production in standard cords, unpeeled, from roundwood by Forest Inventory Unit, county, and species group, Michigan, 2006

Forest Inventory Unit and county[a]	All species	Northern white-cedar	Balsam fir	Hemlock	Jack pine	Red pine	White pine	Spruce	Tamarack	Ash	Aspen/balsam poplar
Eastern Upper Peninsula											
Alger	114,004	99	3,008	4,231	2,663	1,986	378	1,488	526	855	42,102
Chippewa	49,484	33	3,577	2,369	3,335	1,810	520	4,355	136	472	6,105
Delta	99,846	128	4,673	3,238	3,717	2,988	800	2,540	749	985	13,824
Luce	112,364	52	4,414	2,812	9,505	1,455	513	5,556	454	1,015	13,319
Mackinac	61,069	36	2,181	755	4,025	2,367	529	1,341	230	540	19,078
Menominee	82,980	171	6,473	5,095	3,144	2,343	807	3,630	1,747	468	12,544
Schoolcraft	77,047	83	2,504	1,454	3,566	2,974	314	1,226	394	786	13,678
Total	596,793	602	26,831	19,954	29,955	15,923	3,862	20,136	4,236	5,121	120,652
Western Upper Peninsula											
Baraga	117,603	79	2,739	6,113	1,837	1,609	310	2,456	523	1,194	19,759
Dickinson	94,320	95	4,480	1,334	2,348	2,126	432	4,337	1,520	719	11,193
Gogebic	86,176	12	751	1,442	218	159	47	626	191	2,404	10,468
Houghton	83,411	25	1,275	4,188	1,682	2,411	110	561	346	1,607	14,813
Iron	117,826	144	7,041	2,590	4,102	4,031	661	9,230	2,106	1,061	15,111
Keweenaw	46,052	13	432	752	255	224	51	109	98	1,043	2,377
Marquette	220,016	290	9,992	13,949	10,547	4,856	1,225	6,526	2,456	1,100	39,134
Ontonagon	107,261	25	1,403	4,590	804	904	146	1,241	385	2,392	20,226
Total	872,666	683	28,111	34,959	21,794	16,321	2,982	25,088	7,624	11,518	133,079
Northern Lower Peninsula											
Alcona	32,934	--	--	--	902	256	--	--	--	160	25,850
Alpena	19,233	--	297	--	245	23	--	445	--	208	13,453
Antrim	13,377	--	--	--	233	117	--	--	--	296	3,129
Arenac	4,016	--	--	--	391	--	--	--	--	49	1,833
Bay	1,494	--	--	--	29	--	--	--	--	1	903
Benzie	12,197	--	--	--	677	291	--	--	--	270	4,503
Charlevoix	8,962	--	--	--	9	45	--	--	--	40	3,227
Cheboygan	36,608	--	404	--	2,054	406	--	606	--	397	18,011
Clare	38,141	--	--	--	1,362	317	--	--	--	319	26,022
Crawford	30,706	--	7	24	3,148	976	--	27	0	113	14,501
Emmet	14,678	--	--	--	425	447	--	--	--	162	5,250
Gladwin	21,462	--	--	--	728	140	--	--	--	288	11,116
Grand Traverse	6,234	--	--	--	477	502	--	--	--	119	2,218
Iosco	14,311	--	32	22	2,013	759	--	33	10	113	4,930
Isabella	9,171	--	--	--	104	173	--	--	--	21	6,962
Kalkaska	23,870	--	--	--	2,326	1,001	--	--	--	264	8,861
Lake	16,625	--	--	--	1,254	123	--	--	--	282	5,718
Leelanau	1,673	--	--	--	129	155	--	--	--	--	970
Manistee	37,019	--	--	--	1,535	1,862	--	--	--	1,190	12,538
Mason	14,391	--	--	--	617	264	--	--	--	205	8,720

46

County											
Mecosta	14,679	--	--	88	297	476	--	--	--	255	10,177
Midland	5,228	--	--	--	73	115	--	--	--	8	3,554
Missaukee	22,865	--	--	--	930	818	--	--	--	143	13,005
Montmorency	29,797	--	886	--	391	190	314	886	--	373	16,280
Newaygo	3,593	--	--	--	358	513	--	--	--	16	1,926
Oceana	2,291	--	--	--	376	60	--	--	--	18	1,446
Ogemaw	18,635	--	--	--	384	225	--	--	--	156	10,150
Osceola	3,313	--	--	--	--	9	--	--	--	39	2,702
Oscoda	27,380	--	176	--	1,037	522	156	176	--	253	17,493
Otsego	23,821	1	370	7	659	383	158	358	--	286	7,737
Presque Isle	27,937	1	924	15	395	285	61	1,344	5	399	14,903
Roscommon	14,420	--	--	--	1,731	147	--	--	--	65	8,329
Wexford	31,061	--	--	--	882	1,168	--	--	--	883	12,566
Total	**582,121**	**2**	**3,097**	**158**	**26,172**	**12,768**	**689**	**3,876**	**17**	**7,392**	**298,982**
Southern Lower Peninsula											
Allegan	42	--	--	--	--	42	--	--	--	--	--
Barry	482	--	--	--	362	66	--	--	--	--	54
Clinton	933	4	115	126	564	62	15	30	17	--	--
Gratiot	648	--	--	--	--	98	--	--	--	--	550
Huron	381	--	--	--	--	--	--	--	--	--	381
Kent	159	--	--	--	23	--	--	--	--	--	132
Macomb	231	--	--	--	--	--	--	--	--	--	230
Montcalm	2,346	--	--	--	526	47	--	--	--	--	1,325
Muskegon	2,059	--	--	--	--	--	--	--	--	74	1,105
Ottawa	47	--	--	--	47	--	--	--	--	--	--
Sanilac	1,638	--	--	--	18	34	--	--	--	--	1,383
Tuscola	1,821	--	--	--	--	--	--	--	--	--	1,282
Total	**10,787**	**4**	**115**	**126**	**1,539**	**349**	**15**	**30**	**17**	**74**	**6,442**
State total	**2,062,367**	**1,290**	**58,154**	**55,196**	**79,460**	**45,362**	**7,547**	**49,130**	**11,894**	**24,105**	**559,155**

(Table 8 continued on next page)

(Table 8 continued)

| Forest Inventory Unit and county[a] | Species group | | | | | | | | | | White | |
	Basswood	Beech	White birch	Yellow birch	Cotton-wood	Elm	Hickory	Hard maple	Soft maple	Red oak group	oak group	Other hardwoods
Eastern Upper Peninsula												
Alger	863	6,759	3,765	1,931	--	3	--	20,932	18,864	622	--	2,928
Chippewa	339	2,992	1,819	958	--	1	--	10,242	9,517	337	--	566
Delta	1,092	7,870	4,378	2,254	--	3	--	24,282	21,701	727	--	3,897
Luce	636	9,351	3,379	1,805	--	16	--	27,887	28,442	665	--	1,085
Mackinac	476	3,169	2,025	1,088	--	1	--	11,505	10,638	398	--	685
Menominee	2,016	4,862	2,490	1,195	--	5	1	13,216	11,414	397	7	10,953
Schoolcraft	1,256	5,852	3,340	1,728	--	2	--	18,562	16,731	573	--	2,024
Total	6,679	40,855	21,195	10,961	--	32	1	126,627	117,307	3,719	7	22,138
Western Upper Peninsula												
Baraga	1,394	9,846	5,036	2,504	--	6	--	28,230	24,199	861	--	8,909
Dickinson	4,226	3,615	2,606	1,426	1	10	3	15,037	13,931	567	3	24,311
Gogebic	2,117	1,689	3,509	2,094	43	262	87	22,890	31,951	1,094	27	4,096
Houghton	2,377	3,119	3,380	2,327	--	2	--	21,344	11,947	1,601	2	10,296
Iron	1,998	3,027	2,112	1,127	--	11	3	15,280	12,394	421	1	35,374
Keweenaw	873	2,248	2,557	1,666	--	--	--	15,994	14,028	911	1	2,421
Marquette	1,892	16,305	7,252	3,215	--	8	--	38,318	32,432	969	59	29,492
Ontonagon	3,520	2,898	3,936	2,784	3	19	6	26,260	17,994	2,065	--	15,659
Total	18,397	42,746	30,388	17,144	47	318	99	183,352	158,876	8,491	93	130,556
Northern Lower Peninsula												
Alcona	272	151	551	--	--	--	--	621	4,170	--	--	--
Alpena	622	204	451	--	--	--	--	584	2,702	--	--	--
Antrim	2,029	283	674	2	--	--	--	3,845	2,690	--	--	79
Arenac	100	46	87	--	--	--	--	137	1,373	--	--	--
Bay	21	--	--	--	--	--	--	--	540	--	--	--
Benzie	166	247	--	--	--	--	--	2,799	3,074	--	--	169
Charlevoix	2,091	38	--	--	--	--	--	3,266	235	--	--	11
Cheboygan	2,122	472	1,351	104	--	--	--	3,585	6,980	48	--	67
Clare	179	441	--	--	--	--	--	3,484	4,319	1,174	218	306
Crawford	773	102	439	--	--	--	--	1,952	8,643	--	--	--
Emmet	1,272	188	209	30	--	--	--	4,646	2,017	14	--	19
Gladwin	98	263	--	--	--	--	--	1,973	5,962	600	114	181
Grand Traverse	140	109	--	--	--	--	--	1,257	1,338	--	--	75
Iosco	110	106	354	--	--	--	--	352	5,476	--	--	--
Isabella	11	27	--	--	--	--	--	207	1,471	149	27	20
Kalkaska	1,104	267	1,035	4	--	--	--	3,215	5,790	0	--	2
Lake	143	358	--	--	--	--	--	2,756	1,979	3,168	596	248
Leelanau	15	--	--	--	--	--	--	187	218	--	--	--
Manistee	430	1,088	--	--	--	--	--	7,953	4,710	4,170	796	747
Mason	70	187	--	--	--	--	--	1,387	740	1,741	332	128

Mecosta	87	233	--	--	--	--	1,702	1,148	48	9	160
Midland	23	8	--	--	--	--	59	1,383	--	--	5
Missaukee	1,276	131	--	--	--	--	2,728	3,571	146	28	90
Montmorency	2,208	356	795	--	--	--	2,491	4,541	85	--	--
Newaygo	6	15	--	--	--	--	109	192	375	71	10
Oceana	6	17	--	--	--	--	198	145	11	2	11
Ogemaw	147	145	57	--	--	--	1,312	4,355	1,370	261	71
Osceola	13	36	--	--	--	--	261	126	85	16	25
Oscoda	277	234	100	--	--	--	1,575	4,988	224	43	125
Otsego	3,615	350	449	49	--	--	5,586	3,620	87	13	92
Presque Isle	1,023	379	1,219	--	--	--	1,569	5,397	19	--	--
Roscommon	23	59	3	--	--	--	436	3,552	30	6	40
Wexford	301	807	--	--	--	--	6,565	4,002	2,800	534	554
Total	20,772	7,347	7,773	190	--	--	68,797	101,448	16,344	3,066	3,235
Southern Lower Peninsula											
Allegan	--	--	--	--	--	--	--	--	--	--	--
Barry	--	--	--	--	--	--	--	--	--	--	--
Clinton	--	--	--	--	--	--	--	--	--	--	--
Gratiot	--	--	--	--	--	--	--	--	--	--	--
Huron	--	--	--	--	--	--	--	--	--	--	--
Kent	--	--	--	--	--	--	--	5	--	--	--
Macomb	--	--	--	--	--	--	--	0	--	--	--
Montcalm	13	--	--	--	--	--	--	434	--	--	--
Muskegon	25	68	--	--	--	--	498	241	--	--	47
Ottawa	--	--	--	--	--	--	--	--	--	--	--
Sanilac	40	--	--	--	--	--	--	163	--	--	--
Tuscola	--	--	--	--	--	--	--	539	--	--	--
Total	79	68	--	--	--	--	498	1,382	--	--	47
State total	45,926	91,016	59,357	28,294	350	100	379,274	379,013	28,554	3,165	155,976

[a] Includes only those counties that supplied pulpwood in 2006.

All table cells without observations are indicated by -- . Table value of 0 indicates the volume rounds to less than 1 standard cord, unpeeled.

Columns and rows may not add to their totals due to rounding.

Table 9.—Pulpwood production in standard cords, unpeeled, from roundwood by Forest Inventory Unit, county, and species group, Minnesota, 2006

Forest Inventory Unit and county[a]	All species	Species group								
		Balsam fir	Jack pine	Red pine	White pine	Spruce	Tamarack	Other softwoods	Ash	Aspen/ balsam poplar
Aspen-Birch										
Carlton	61,443	4,510	957	2,288	35	1,797	199	--	1,329	37,255
Cook	19,722	782	170	416	2	3,935	5	--	38	13,572
Koochiching	324,539	29,477	14,415	612	116	54,907	8,646	--	653	192,202
Lake	72,056	10,182	2,532	3,411	22	11,953	197	--	736	31,198
St. Louis	550,814	49,933	19,038	7,419	401	63,826	12,793	--	4,085	317,519
Total	1,028,573	94,883	37,111	14,147	576	136,419	21,839	--	6,841	591,747
Northern Pine										
Aitkin	132,821	4,544	1,818	887	178	3,964	659	--	1,526	93,396
Becker	48,452	3,636	2,632	255	0	957	168	--	24	36,014
Beltrami	151,841	13,477	8,705	878	5	5,254	1,681	--	1,311	108,333
Cass	147,863	3,293	10,087	1,587	118	2,491	449	--	573	106,343
Cleanwater	67,286	3,291	3,912	611	0	2,226	118	--	85	50,745
Crow Wing	97,549	142	5,031	811	48	166	127	--	1,003	69,812
Hubbard	94,531	2,719	13,258	3,163	45	1,156	107	--	42	64,942
Itasca	266,865	28,073	6,570	1,925	75	30,294	3,671	0	1,892	167,859
Lake of the Woods	64,044	3,787	5,239	184	0	5,256	3,574	--	118	40,298
Mahnomen	10,566	100	207	87	--	125	77	--	5	9,617
Roseau	41,339	624	3,057	524	--	5,495	1,000	--	12	28,542
Wadena	37,558	134	14,473	756	2	13	--	9	--	21,718
Total	1,160,713	63,819	74,988	11,668	473	57,396	11,629	9	6,591	797,619

Central Hardwood

Anoka	300	--	176	45	2	--	--	--	--	54
Benton	1,270	--	60	74	42	6	--	--	52	751
Chisago	365	--	2	15	--	--	--	--	2	229
Douglas	103	--	14	--	--	--	--	--	--	89
Goodhue	63	--	--	--	--	--	--	--	--	63
Houston	321	--	--	316	--	--	--	--	--	0
Isanti	1,305	--	34	130	--	--	--	--	11	1,059
Kanabec	24,245	20	221	129	10	8	39	--	215	19,746
Mille Lacs	15,401	11	120	56	5	5	15	--	145	12,734
Morrison	28,002	9	192	96	5	20	12	12	114	25,693
Otter Tail	17,937	6	117	246	--	--	--	88	23	17,172
Pine	89,188	1,584	1,774	2,413	42	456	104	--	915	61,723
Sherburne	439	0	49	176	--	6	0	--	4	138
Stearns	275	--	1	0	--	--	--	--	1	255
Todd	5,135	--	99	25	--	--	--	728	--	4,153
Wabasha	238	--	--	13	81	62	--	--	--	81
Washington	117	--	3	1	--	--	0	--	3	73
Winona	125	--	--	--	53	--	--	--	1	18
Wright	198	0	5	2	--	--	0	--	4	125
Total	185,027	1,631	2,868	3,737	240	564	171	829	1,490	144,156

Prairie

Kittson	42,337	86	338	--	--	245	156	--	58	40,914
Marshall	10,845	22	85	--	--	61	39	--	--	10,517
Norman	2,278	--	--	--	--	--	--	--	--	2,268
Pennington	1,449	--	--	--	--	--	--	--	--	1,449
Polk	7,981	--	--	--	--	--	--	--	23	7,917
Red Lake	2,654	--	--	--	--	--	--	--	--	2,654
Total	67,544	108	423	--	--	307	195	--	82	65,718
State total	2,441,857	160,441	115,389	29,551	1,289	194,685	33,834	838	15,004	1,599,240

(Table 9 continued on next page)

(Table 9 continued)

Forest Inventory Unit and county[a]	Species group								
	Basswood	White birch	Cotton-wood	Elm	Hard maple	Soft maple	Red oak group	White oak group	Other hardwoods
Aspen-Birch									
Carlton	474	4,759	--	--	1,908	5,931	--	--	--
Cook	19	433	--	--	80	271	--	--	--
Koochiching	256	22,407	--	--	61	788	--	--	--
Lake	709	5,639	--	--	1,172	4,305	--	--	--
St. Louis	1,522	42,764	--	--	9,658	21,855	--	--	--
Total	2,980	76,001	--	--	12,879	33,151	--	--	--
Northern Pine									
Aitkin	1,229	9,740	--	--	2,855	11,959	47	19	--
Becker	273	2,913	--	--	1,116	462	--	--	--
Beltrami	1,043	6,985	--	--	2,305	1,866	--	--	--
Cass	1,314	12,015	--	--	1,309	8,284	--	--	--
Clearwater	450	3,726	--	--	1,558	563	--	--	--
Crow Wing	1,092	7,484	--	--	2,142	9,683	5	2	--
Hubbard	666	6,491	--	--	411	1,532	--	--	--
Itasca	1,476	16,357	--	--	1,232	7,442	--	--	--
Lake of the Woods	12	5,443	--	--	30	103	--	--	--
Mahnomen	6	268	3	--	70	1	--	--	--
Roseau	--	2,085	--	--	--	--	--	--	--
Wadena	7	391	--	--	--	55	--	--	--
Total	7,568	73,900	3	--	13,028	41,951	52	21	--

Central Hardwood

County									
Anoka	--	23	--	--	--	--	--	--	--
Benton	151	40	29	65	--	--	--	--	--
Chisago	76	20	4	15	--	--	--	--	--
Douglas	--	--	--	--	--	--	--	--	--
Goodhue	--	--	--	--	--	--	--	--	--
Houston	1	--	--	1	--	--	2	1	--
Isanti	23	12	20	--	--	--	12	5	--
Kanabec	459	1,374	441	1,583	--	--	--	--	--
Mille Lacs	120	608	349	1,189	--	--	32	13	--
Morrison	80	626	227	894	--	--	17	7	--
Otter Tail	157	69	59	--	--	--	--	--	--
Pine	825	7,834	4,274	7,215	--	--	20	8	--
Sherburne	2	29	8	26	--	--	--	--	--
Stearns	1	6	3	9	--	--	--	--	--
Todd	55	74	--	--	--	--	--	--	--
Wabasha	--	--	--	--	--	--	--	--	--
Washington	1	12	5	18	--	--	--	--	--
Winona	3	2	30	--	5	--	6	3	0
Wright	2	20	9	31	--	--	--	--	--
Total	1,954	10,749	5,456	11,046	5	5	90	37	0

Prairie

County									
Kittson	--	538	--	0	--	--	--	--	--
Marshall	--	121	--	--	--	--	--	--	--
Norman	--	10	--	--	--	--	--	--	--
Pennington	--	--	--	--	--	--	--	--	--
Polk	--	--	30	10	--	--	--	--	--
Red Lake	--	--	--	--	--	--	--	--	--
Total	--	670	30	10	--	--	--	--	--
State total	12,503	161,320	31,393	86,157	8	5	142	58	0

[a] Includes only those counties that supplied pulpwood in 2006. Table value of 0 indicates the volume rounds to less than 1 standard cord, unpeeled. All table cells without observations are indicated by -- .
Columns and rows may not add to their totals due to rounding.

Table 10.—Pulpwood production in standard cords, unpeeled, from roundwood by Forest Inventory Unit, county, and species group, Wisconsin, 2006

Forest inventory Unit and county[a]	All species	Northern white-cedar	Balsam fir	Hemlock	Jack pine	Red pine	White pine	Other pines	Spruce	Tamarack	Ash	Aspen/ balsam poplar
Northeastern												
Florence	55,799	15	2,248	2,729	843	1,428	198	--	7,239	387	559	10,143
Forest	89,509	6	4,558	1,180	308	4,933	290	--	25,320	698	1,663	7,122
Langlade	124,034	--	5,339	317	168	2,036	159	--	5,334	605	3,390	36,454
Lincoln	91,242	--	3,849	329	429	1,202	798	--	1,623	324	2,851	42,036
Marinette	123,265	8	3,987	2,342	8,712	6,248	864	--	1,747	1,325	1,846	23,131
Menominee	32,142	--	17	3,338	176	794	211	--	2	1	1,520	6,681
Oconto	45,844	--	682	112	1,164	6,515	654	--	421	176	1,408	13,794
Oneida	108,772	--	5,317	305	4,900	10,853	900	--	7,143	606	1,076	49,900
Shawano	35,525	--	1,413	909	283	2,176	193	--	230	182	2,590	6,848
Vilas	50,951	--	2,764	347	6,209	1,895	1,643	--	1,459	437	631	20,063
Total	757,084	30	30,174	11,906	23,193	38,079	5,909	--	50,517	4,743	17,533	216,173
Northwestern												
Ashland	156,276	--	8,845	192	2,460	2,249	1,771	--	4,345	318	2,720	51,375
Barron	15,720	--	107	--	25	513	142	--	68	19	280	9,338
Bayfield	121,075	--	4,484	106	2,371	2,869	746	--	2,595	58	1,686	56,454
Burnett	42,847	--	240	1,011	1,301	1,369	108	--	22	2	528	20,668
Douglas	107,012	--	3,591	122	9,705	7,077	430	--	868	196	1,342	40,090
Iron	47,931	--	3,202	48	506	746	211	--	1,286	33	634	22,390
Polk	9,677	--	49	--	64	109	52	--	--	--	96	6,804
Price	81,255	--	8,568	416	145	863	554	--	5,467	331	1,030	41,442
Rusk	54,358	--	655	17	75	216	126	--	3,063	16	1,724	29,633
Sawyer	149,559	--	4,355	202	1,988	3,753	1,423	--	3,306	953	3,422	72,780
Taylor	35,842	--	1,989	662	23	406	117	--	1,854	117	1,006	19,803
Washburn	74,396	--	1,354	256	9,716	3,701	434	--	246	167	621	38,322
Total	895,947	--	37,440	3,032	28,380	23,870	6,112	--	23,121	2,210	15,089	409,099
Central												
Adams	85,193	--	--	2	8,354	21,490	6,381	--	2,196	--	146	9,195
Chippewa	24,763	--	6	3	634	1,592	657	--	744	0	346	16,877
Clark	48,223	--	--	--	432	774	1,430	--	1,064	191	548	36,061
Eau Claire	16,800	--	18	--	3,112	2,779	1,857	--	50	50	82	5,249
Jackson	37,183	--	--	--	2,268	3,286	4,610	--	195	1,815	22	10,061
Juneau	28,135	--	--	--	4,511	4,605	4,691	--	--	849	142	4,083
Marathon	72,055	--	774	1,558	238	2,768	579	--	1,201	38	2,338	40,890
Marquette	16,918	--	--	--	1,113	4,984	1,272	--	114	478	108	1,482
Monroe	16,406	--	7	--	1,445	2,637	2,546	--	16	669	106	2,324
Portage	40,632	--	202	1,107	1,411	8,782	2,674	--	5,916	348	505	13,484
Waupaca	17,007	--	247	131	71	1,647	938	--	176	194	810	6,882
Waushara	20,875	--	16	--	487	9,250	3,129	21	458	700	251	1,573
Wood	35,471	--	3	159	1,338	9,349	4,978	--	1,027	297	178	13,303
Total	459,659	--	1,273	2,960	25,414	73,941	35,742	21	13,157	5,580	5,583	161,464

Southwestern

County												
Buffalo	1,665	–	–	–	–	–	240	25	181	–	14	653
Crawford	191	–	–	–	–	–	–	–	17	–	–	174
Dunn	13,945	–	–	–	–	506	1,924	894	106	74	175	5,083
Grant	684	–	–	–	–	16	409	52	–	–	5	65
Iowa	2,573	–	–	–	–	56	188	677	50	–	34	743
La Crosse	4,085	–	–	–	–	281	794	1,461	66	–	10	773
Lafayette	1,285	–	–	–	–	–	–	–	–	–	184	3
Pepin	1,206	–	–	–	–	54	516	126	58	–	5	270
Pierce	760	–	–	–	–	40	164	71	6	–	1	399
Richland	4,151	–	–	–	–	–	583	914	453	–	47	1,410
Sauk	6,808	–	–	–	–	729	3,089	384	–	–	91	432
St Croix	7,704	–	–	–	2	847	2,064	421	604	–	11	3,248
Trempealeau	4,646	–	–	–	–	38	674	934	–	–	33	572
Vernon	1,545	–	–	–	–	–	–	476	236	–	37	377
Total	**51,247**	–	–	–	**2**	**2,569**	**10,644**	**6,436**	**1,778**	**74**	**647**	**14,200**

Southeastern

County												
Brown	1,782	–	–	–	–	17	441	76	–	–	253	362
Calumet	563	–	–	–	–	–	10	3	–	13	122	28
Columbia	11,992	–	–	–	–	31	5,114	648	273	112	146	2,497
Dane	2,660	–	–	–	–	–	358	393	422	–	281	181
Dodge	547	–	–	–	–	–	24	16	19	–	255	9
Door	4,010	–	–	86	–	–	226	383	142	–	232	298
Fond Du Lac	2,969	–	–	–	–	–	210	96	99	18	62	468
Green	321	–	–	15	–	–	24	55	–	–	89	–
Green Lake	11,656	–	–	–	–	146	889	488	96	21	36	8,590
Jefferson	61	–	–	–	–	–	16	–	–	–	–	36
Kewaunee	2,615	–	–	57	19	–	134	44	142	116	613	221
Manitowoc	2,009	–	–	–	45	–	44	149	340	16	447	82
Outagamie	3,724	–	–	–	–	–	320	55	22	99	793	870
Ozaukee	10	–	–	–	–	–	–	–	–	–	–	–
Rock	535	–	–	–	–	119	24	75	89	–	24	60
Sheboygan	829	–	–	–	–	–	74	360	9	–	135	–
Walworth	499	–	–	–	–	–	221	206	72	–	–	–
Washington	529	–	–	–	–	108	308	75	–	–	10	–
Waukesha	880	–	–	–	–	–	583	240	–	–	32	–
Winnebago	347	–	–	–	–	–	84	15	27	–	5	189
Total	**48,538**	–	–	**157**	**64**	**421**	**9,104**	**3,376**	**1,753**	**397**	**3,534**	**13,891**
State total	**2,212,475**	**30**	**21**	**69,046**	**17,963**	**79,976**	**155,639**	**57,574**	**90,326**	**13,005**	**42,387**	**814,827**

(Table 10 continued on next page)

(Table 10 continued)

						Species group						
Forest Inventory Unit and county[a]	Basswood	Beech	White birch	Yellow birch	Cotton-wood	Elm	Hickory	Hard maple	Soft maple	Red oak group	White oak group	Other hardwoods
Northeastern												
Florence	1,279	1,352	1,342	916	--	--	--	9,270	8,287	531	7	7,027
Forest	1,656	1,803	2,020	1,294	11	63	20	17,399	13,575	653	17	4,920
Langlade	4,177	2,868	3,098	1,986	19	114	31	31,468	23,190	980	23	2,278
Lincoln	2,389	287	2,261	1,475	93	555	184	19,465	10,591	353	40	107
Marinette	7,169	1,626	2,745	1,710	1	4	1	16,742	12,612	2,753	44	27,647
Menominee	904	859	293	1,308	6	41	11	10,378	4,999	503	41	58
Oconto	403	730	779	482	--	--	--	5,410	6,161	578	9	6,368
Oneida	889	910	1,880	1,179	41	254	82	10,697	8,632	1,311	114	1,783
Shawano	584	119	136	106	39	292	7	8,719	6,191	1,030	125	3,353
Vilas	167	105	897	576	32	190	63	4,865	2,871	1,198	125	4,413
Total	19,617	10,660	15,452	11,032	242	1,514	399	134,413	97,108	9,890	545	57,956
Northwestern												
Ashland	3,997	119	7,705	82	--	3	1	15,786	51,572	2,401	248	87
Barron	501	3	435	50	3	39	6	849	1,571	1,587	183	--
Bayfield	3,690	8	4,699	117	7	38	12	9,562	27,196	3,931	446	--
Burnett	462	--	1,339	2	--	20	--	2,002	6,622	6,403	749	--
Douglas	1,898	--	7,599	4	--	1	--	9,623	24,124	309	33	--
Iron	1,223	181	1,671	319	13	80	27	4,654	9,746	79	1	883
Polk	400	--	331	2	--	6	--	265	547	837	114	--
Price	1,146	475	1,915	1,081	52	315	103	8,824	7,985	356	26	162
Rusk	3,775	25	2,137	125	7	124	14	4,568	6,167	1,683	205	--
Sawyer	7,259	264	2,832	291	3	89	7	11,988	24,305	9,172	1,063	105
Taylor	275	80	501	166	10	86	20	5,337	3,242	129	14	6
Washburn	2,504	4	1,140	53	3	39	6	2,626	7,778	4,748	675	1
Total	27,131	1,159	32,304	2,292	98	840	196	76,083	170,852	31,635	3,756	1,245
Central												
Adams	2	5	112	75	5	50	9	395	1,690	30,959	4,128	--
Chippewa	252	3	806	8	1	11	1	644	1,176	890	111	--
Clark	211	32	120	29	--	62	3	2,238	2,560	2,110	355	3
Eau Claire	56	4	77	11	1	33	1	243	1,244	1,711	271	--
Jackson	2	3	56	34	--	160	4	186	2,624	10,191	1,665	--
Juneau	3	8	193	126	8	87	16	755	1,206	5,786	1,066	--
Marathon	271	232	227	90	5	60	10	13,636	6,684	411	30	18
Marquette	12	5	118	62	4	40	7	335	426	5,630	729	--
Monroe	10	--	17	1	5	45	--	128	712	4,808	931	--
Portage	1	44	128	16	1	24	1	2,430	1,989	1,395	165	7
Waupaca	--	47	39	27	4	18	--	3,075	2,037	577	85	--
Waushara	--	1	20	53	--	5	2	66	559	3,822	459	1
Wood	20	12	101	49	3	41	6	687	1,319	2,207	389	6
Total	838	396	2,015	582	38	636	60	24,818	24,225	70,498	10,384	35

Southwestern

County												
Buffalo	6	2	17	8	5	14	1	45	146	270	37	--
Crawford	--	--	--	--	--	--	--	--	--	--	--	3
Dunn	25	5	113	26	0	60	3	421	596	3,509	421	--
Grant	--	--	--	--	1	14	--	25	37	51	10	--
Iowa	6	--	3	--	--	112	--	91	403	160	50	--
La Crosse	19	--	31	5	--	15	1	49	96	409	77	--
Lafayette	--	--	--	3	--	16	--	578	427	73	3	1
Pepin	--	1	9	--	--	2	--	24	19	103	12	--
Pierce	1	--	1	--	--	1	--	7	10	53	7	--
Richland	20	1	11	--	16	57	--	337	127	134	42	--
Sauk	2	1	25	16	12	29	--	130	360	1,284	223	--
St Croix	20	--	24	5	--	--	1	73	135	226	24	--
Trempealeau	3	3	77	48	21	35	6	250	319	1,455	178	--
Vernon	6	--	2	--	18	37	--	156	138	44	19	--
Total	**105**	**12**	**313**	**111**	**75**	**393**	**12**	**2,186**	**2,812**	**7,770**	**1,103**	**4**

Southeastern

County												
Brown	--	6	30	14	0	1	1	120	273	11	1	175
Calumet	--	6	12	1	--	1	--	14	340	11	1	--
Columbia	--	2	44	14	7	19	--	110	484	2,135	353	--
Dane	1	--	0	--	5	51	--	128	577	228	35	--
Dodge	--	--	--	--	--	--	--	--	225	--	--	--
Door	--	34	328	71	2	12	2	352	147	1,337	149	208
Fond Du Lac	2	2	46	31	8	16	2	248	137	1,367	155	--
Green	--	--	--	--	--	--	--	40	98	--	--	--
Green Lake	1	3	5	4	--	23	--	241	549	490	74	--
Jefferson	--	--	--	--	--	--	--	--	--	8	1	--
Kewaunee	10	6	17	5	--	10	--	185	887	82	12	56
Manitowoc	5	65	2	45	--	--	--	387	306	22	1	54
Outagamie	--	39	136	3	5	3	--	113	1,128	7	1	131
Ozaukee	--	--	10	--	--	--	--	--	--	--	--	--
Rock	--	--	--	--	--	--	--	7	127	11	11	--
Sheboygan	--	53	10	10	--	3	--	106	57	11	1	--
Walworth	--	--	--	--	--	--	1	--	--	--	--	--
Washington	--	--	1	1	--	--	--	16	9	--	--	--
Waukesha	--	--	--	--	--	--	--	8	6	11	1	--
Winnebago	--	--	3	2	--	--	--	9	14	--	--	--
Total	**19**	**216**	**646**	**202**	**28**	**140**	**6**	**2,083**	**5,364**	**5,729**	**784**	**625**
State total	**47,710**	**12,443**	**50,730**	**14,218**	**481**	**3,523**	**673**	**239,584**	**300,361**	**125,521**	**16,572**	**59,865**

[a] Includes only those counties that supplied pulpwood in 2006.

All table cells without observations are indicated by --. Table value of 0 indicates the volume rounds to less than 1 standard cord, unpeeled.

Columns and rows may not add to their totals due to rounding.

Table 11.—Average production of active wood-pulp and composite product mills by company, location, and type of product produced, Lake States, 2006

Product and company	Location	Product produced	Average production
Pulp mills			
New Page Corp.	Escanaba, MI	Kraft/groundwood pulp	1,125 tons pulp/day
Packaging Corp. Of America	Filer City, MI	Semichemical pulp	361 tons pulp/day
Smurfit-Stone Container Corp.	Ontonagon, MI	Semichemical pulp	751 tons pulp/day
Verso Paper	Quinnesec, MI	Kraft pulp	1,250 tons pulp/day
Boise White Paper, LLC.	International Falls, MN	Kraft pulp	1,150 tons pulp/day
Certainteed Corp.	Shakopee, MN	Groundwood/mechanical pulp	310 tons pulp/day
Sapppi, LLC	Cloquet, MN	Kraft pulp	1,400 tons pulp/day
Stora Enso North America	Proctor, MN	Groundwood/mechanical pulp	325 tons pulp/day
UPM - Blandin	Grand Rapids, MN	Groundwood/mechanical pulp	475 tons pulp/day
Verso Paper	Sartell, MN	Thermomechanical pulp	850 tons pulp/day
Domtar Industries, Inc.	Nekoosa, WI	Kraft pulp	495 tons pulp/day
Domtar Industries, Inc.	Port Edwards, WI	Sulfite pulp	255 tons pulp/day
Mule-Hide Manufacturing	Cornell, WI	Thermomechanical pulp	130 tons pulp/day
Packaging Corp. Of America	Tomahawk, WI	Semichemical pulpw	1,350 tons pulp/day
Stora Enso North America	Biron, WI	Groundwood/mechanical pulp	400 tons pulp/day
Stora Enso North America	Niagara, WI	Groundwood/mechanical pulp	250 tons pulp/day
Stora Enso North America	Stevens Point, WI	Thermomechanical pulp	200 tons pulp/day
Thilmany, LLC	Kaukauna, WI	Kraft pulp	400 tons pulp/day
Wausau Mosinee Paper	Mosinee, WI	Kraft pulp	212 tons pulp/day
Weyerhaeuser Co.	Rothschild, WI	Sulfite pulp	160 tons pulp/day

Composite product mills

Decorative Panels International, Inc.	Alpena, MI	Hardboard	120 million ft^2, 3/4-inch basis per year
Louisiana-Pacific Corp.	Newberry, MI	Oriented strand board	72 million ft^2, 3/4-inch basis per year
Louisiana-Pacific Corp.	Sagola, MI	Oriented strand board	201 million ft^2, 3/4-inch basis per year
Weyerhaeuser Co.	Grayling, MI	Oriented strand board	250 million ft^2, 3/4-inch basis per year
Ainsworth Engineered (USA), LLC	Bemidji, MN	Oriented strand board	234 million ft^2, 3/4-inch basis per year
Ainsworth Engineered (USA), LLC	Cook, MN	Oriented strand board	159 million ft^2, 3/4-inch basis per year
Ainsworth Engineered (USA), LLC	Grand Rapids, MN	Oriented strand board	97 million ft^2, 3/4-inch basis per year
Georgia-Pacific Corp.	Duluth, MN	Hardboard	220 million ft^2, 3/4-inch basis per year
International Bildrite, Inc.	International Falls, MN	Medium density fiberboard	59 million ft^2, 3/4-inch basis per year
Louisiana-Pacific Corp.	Two Harbors, MN	Oriented strand board	75 million ft^2, 3/4-inch basis per year
Norbord Minnesota	Solway, MN	Oriented strand board	456 million ft^2, 3/4-inch basis per year
Trus Joist by Weyerhaeuser	Deerwood, MN	Engineered wood product	na
Georgia-Pacific Corp., LLC	Phillips, WI	Hardboard	85 million ft^2, 3/4-inch basis per year
Louisiana-Pacific Corp.	Hayward, WI	Oriented strand board	210 million ft^2, 3/4-inch basis per year
Louisiana-Pacific Corp.	Tomahawk, WI	Oriented strand board	66 million ft^2, 3/4-inch basis per year
Marshfield Doorsystems, Inc.	Marshfield, WI	Particleboard	79 million ft^2, 3/4-inch basis per year

Table 12.—Production and imports of pulpwood in standard cords, unpeeled, Mid-Atlantic States, 2006

Product form, species group, and destination	Production by state[a]								Imports					Total receipts
	Delaware	Maryland	New Jersey	New York	Ohio	Pennsyl-vania	West Virginia	Regional Total	Central States	New England States	Southern States	Canada	Total imports	
Softwood roundwood														
Balsam fir														
Canada	--	--	--	58	--	--	--	58	--	--	--	--	--	--
Mid-Atlantic States	--	--	--	9,570	--	--	--	9,570	--	6,918	--	295	7,212	16,782
New England States	--	--	--	180	--	--	--	180	--	--	--	--	--	--
Total	--	--	--	9,808	--	--	--	9,808	--	6,918	--	295	7,212	16,782
Hemlock														
Canada	--	--	--	64	--	--	--	64	--	--	--	--	--	--
Mid-Atlantic States	--	332	--	78,987	4,314	50,405	3,053	137,090	--	46,708	1,778	1,736	50,222	187,311
New England States	--	--	--	365	--	--	--	365	--	--	--	--	--	--
Southern States	--	--	--	--	--	--	681	681	--	--	--	--	--	--
Total	--	332	--	79,415	4,314	50,405	3,734	138,200	--	46,708	1,778	1,736	50,222	187,311
Shortleaf/loblolly pine														
Mid-Atlantic States	19,881	31,257	--	--	1,650	358	3,345	56,509	1,425	--	40,751	--	42,176	98,685
Southern States	--	106	--	--	--	--	34	140	--	--	--	--	--	--
Total	19,881	31,362	--	--	1,650	358	3,379	56,649	1,425	--	40,751	--	42,176	98,685
Red pine														
Mid-Atlantic States	--	582	--	1,547	3,934	4,797	80	10,940	--	--	44	--	44	10,983
New England States	--	--	--	33	--	--	--	33	--	--	--	--	--	--
Total	--	582	--	1,580	3,934	4,797	80	10,972	--	--	44	--	44	10,983
White pine														
Canada	--	--	--	8,365	--	--	--	8,365	--	--	--	--	--	--
Mid-Atlantic States	--	1,863	16	57,239	45,596	38,463	19,402	162,577	205	14,103	17,116	--	31,424	194,001
New England States	--	--	--	569	--	--	--	569	--	--	--	--	--	--
Southern States	--	--	--	--	--	--	1,482	1,482	--	--	--	--	--	--
Total	--	1,863	16	66,173	45,596	38,463	20,885	172,994	205	14,103	17,116	--	31,424	194,001
Other pines														
Canada	--	--	--	136	--	--	--	136	--	--	--	--	--	--
Mid-Atlantic States	2,618	19,457	5,475	428	41,538	24,269	51,110	144,894	1,912	15,655	93,772	689	95,684	240,578
New England States	--	--	--	13	--	--	--	13	--	--	--	--	--	--
Southern States	--	47	--	--	--	--	909	956	--	--	--	--	--	--
Total	2,618	19,503	5,475	578	41,538	24,269	52,019	145,999	1,912	15,655	93,772	689	95,684	240,578
Spruce														
Canada	--	--	--	247	--	--	--	247	--	--	--	--	--	--
Mid-Atlantic States	--	150	1	22,625	--	5,655	878	29,309	--	15,655	542	689	16,885	46,194
New England States	--	--	--	276	--	--	--	276	--	--	--	--	--	--
Southern States	--	--	--	--	--	--	193	193	--	--	--	--	--	--
Total	--	150	1	23,147	--	5,655	1,071	30,025	--	15,655	542	689	16,885	46,194
Tamarack														
Mid-Atlantic States	--	--	--	--	--	285	--	285	--	--	--	--	--	285
Total	--	--	--	--	--	285	--	285	--	--	--	--	--	285

Total softwood roundwood

Canada	22,499	--	--	8,870	--	--	--	8,870	--	--	--	--	--	8,870
Mid-Atlantic States	--	53,639	5,510	170,395	97,031	124,231	77,868	551,174	3,542	83,383	154,002	2,719	243,646	781,064
New England States	--	--	--	1,435	--	--	--	1,435	--	--	--	--	--	1,435
Southern States	--	153	--	--	--	--	3,300	3,452	--	--	--	--	--	3,452
Total	22,499	53,792	5,510	180,701	97,031	124,231	81,168	564,932	3,542	83,383	154,002	2,719	243,646	794,821

Softwood residues

Mid-Atlantic States	--	37,334	--	14,610	8,848	189,155	1,912	251,858	480	10,336	32,849	--	43,665	295,523
Southern States	--	46,757	--	--	--	--	5,236	51,993	--	--	--	--	--	--
Total	--	84,091	--	14,610	8,848	189,155	7,147	303,851	480	10,336	32,849	--	43,665	295,523

Total softwood material

Canada	22,499	--	--	8,870	--	--	--	8,870	--	--	--	--	--	8,870
Mid-Atlantic States	--	90,973	5,510	185,005	105,879	313,386	79,780	803,033	4,022	93,719	186,851	2,719	287,311	1,076,587
New England States	--	--	--	1,435	--	--	--	1,435	--	--	--	--	--	1,435
Southern States	--	46,910	--	--	--	--	8,535	55,445	--	--	--	--	--	3,452
Total	22,499	137,883	5,510	195,311	105,879	313,386	88,315	868,783	4,022	93,719	186,851	2,719	287,311	1,090,344

(Table 12 continued on next page)

(Table 12 continued)

Product form, species group, and destination	Production by state[a]								Imports					Total receipts
	Delaware	Maryland	New Jersey	New York	Ohio	Pennsylvania	West Virginia	Regional Total	Central States	New England States	Southern States	Canada	Total imports	
Hardwood roundwood														
Ash														
Canada	--	--	--	10,228	--	--	--	10,228	--	--	--	--	--	--
Mid-Atlantic States	18	1,629	--	23,442	12,581	26,939	4,495	69,105	0	1,615	568	--	2,184	71,289
Southern States	--	9	--	--	--	116	4,574	4,700	--	--	--	--	--	--
Total	18	1,638	--	33,670	12,581	27,056	9,070	84,033	0	1,615	568	--	2,184	71,289
Aspen/balsam poplar														
Canada	--	--	--	2,977	--	--	--	2,977	--	--	--	--	--	--
Mid-Atlantic States	11	187	--	17,053	7,910	11,874	4,561	41,596	--	627	645	--	1,272	42,867
New England States	--	--	--	61	--	--	--	61	--	--	--	--	--	--
Southern States	--	14	--	--	--	75	--	88	--	--	--	--	--	--
Total	11	200	--	20,091	7,910	11,949	4,561	44,722	--	627	645	--	1,272	42,867
Basswood														
Canada	--	--	--	921	--	--	--	921	--	--	--	--	--	--
Mid-Atlantic States	--	3,103	--	2,109	3,998	13,058	36,800	59,068	--	--	13,156	--	13,156	72,224
Southern States	--	--	--	--	--	81	7,224	7,305	--	--	--	--	--	--
Total	--	3,103	--	3,030	3,998	13,138	44,025	67,294	--	--	13,156	--	13,156	72,224
Beech														
Canada	--	--	--	14,272	--	--	--	14,272	--	--	--	--	--	--
Mid-Atlantic States	64	1,179	--	38,369	7,956	21,931	17,944	87,443	1	2,679	4,236	--	6,915	94,359
Southern States	--	170	--	--	--	131	5,301	5,601	--	--	--	--	--	--
Total	64	1,349	--	52,641	7,956	22,061	23,244	107,317	1	2,679	4,236	--	6,915	94,359
White birch														
Canada	--	--	--	5,077	--	--	--	5,077	--	--	--	--	--	--
Mid-Atlantic States	--	--	--	19,931	--	929	--	20,859	--	1,904	--	--	1,904	22,763
Total	--	--	--	25,008	--	929	--	25,936	--	1,904	--	--	1,904	22,763
Yellow birch														
Canada	--	--	--	7,677	--	--	--	7,677	--	--	--	--	--	--
Mid-Atlantic States	--	203	--	30,842	32	4,660	2,419	38,157	--	2,499	6	--	2,505	40,662
Southern States	--	13	--	--	--	38	2,690	2,741	--	--	--	--	--	--
Total	--	216	--	38,519	32	4,698	5,109	48,575	--	2,499	6	--	2,505	40,662
Other birch														
Canada	--	--	--	149	--	--	--	149	--	--	--	--	--	--
Mid-Atlantic States	--	991	--	928	467	27,399	14,695	44,479	1	--	2,088	--	2,088	46,568
Southern States	--	--	--	--	--	79	4,278	4,357	--	--	--	--	--	--
Total	--	991	--	1,077	467	27,478	18,973	48,986	1	--	2,088	--	2,088	46,568
Black cherry														
Canada	--	--	--	1,005	--	--	--	1,005	--	--	--	--	--	--
Mid-Atlantic States	42	7,105	--	17,436	13,546	85,813	10,746	134,688	1	726	337	--	1,064	135,751
Southern States	--	--	--	--	--	--	8,298	8,298	--	--	--	--	--	--
Total	42	7,105	--	18,441	13,546	85,813	19,044	143,990	1	726	337	--	1,064	135,751
Black walnut														
Mid-Atlantic States	--	89	--	--	1,496	1,023	82	2,691	--	--	27	--	27	2,718
Total	--	89	--	--	1,496	1,023	82	2,691	--	--	27	--	27	2,718
Cottonwood														
Mid-Atlantic States	--	127	--	--	1,352	178	--	1,657	--	--	71	--	71	1,728
Total	--	127	--	--	1,352	178	--	1,657	--	--	71	--	71	1,728

Table 12 (continued)

Species / Region												
Elm												
Canada	--	--	--	248	--	--	248	--	--	--	--	--
Mid-Atlantic States	9	855	8,089	97	3,535	5,016	17,602	1	--	1,161	1,162	18,763
Southern States	--	1	--	--	21	585	607	--	--	--	--	--
Total	9	856	8,089	344	3,556	5,601	18,456	1	--	1,161	1,162	18,763
Hickory												
Canada	--	--	--	--	--	--	--	--	--	--	--	--
Mid-Atlantic States	12	2,749	--	19,289	11,412	9,500	42,963	3	--	1,206	1,206	44,172
Southern States	--	56	--	31	8,961	9,048	--	--	--	--	--	--
Total	12	2,804	--	19,289	11,444	18,462	52,011	3	--	1,206	1,209	44,172
Hard maple												
Canada	--	44,863	--	--	--	44,863	--	--	--	--	--	--
Mid-Atlantic States	3,801	68,903	18,200	51,251	11,062	153,218	1	5,109	1,020	6,130	159,348	
Southern States	--	305	11,003	11,308	--	--	--	--	--	--	--	--
Total	3,801	113,766	18,200	51,556	22,065	209,389	1	5,109	1,020	6,130	159,348	
Soft maple												
Canada	1,735	13,618	--	--	--	13,618	--	--	--	--	--	--
Mid-Atlantic States	14,559	69,382	31,849	147,213	98,142	362,882	4	4,592	32,861	37,458	400,340	
Southern States	261	--	696	19,682	20,639	--	--	--	--	--	--	--
Total	14,820	83,000	31,849	147,909	117,824	397,139	4	4,592	32,861	37,458	400,340	
Red oak group												
Canada	--	1,150	--	--	--	1,150	--	--	--	--	--	--
Mid-Atlantic States	13,117	21,563	22,195	75,259	25,204	158,187	8	1,185	2,321	3,514	161,701	
Southern States	356	--	199	22,391	22,946	--	--	--	--	--	--	--
Total	13,473	22,712	22,195	75,458	47,594	182,282	8	1,185	2,321	3,514	161,701	
White oak group												
Canada	--	61	--	--	--	61	--	--	--	--	--	--
Mid-Atlantic States	14,055	6,934	35,508	70,048	34,535	161,712	8	438	3,296	3,742	165,454	
Southern States	308	--	107	32,876	33,290	--	--	--	--	--	--	--
Total	14,362	6,995	35,508	70,154	67,410	195,063	8	438	3,296	3,742	165,454	
Sweetgum												
Canada	670	2,896	--	171	16	78	3,830	--	--	421	421	4,251
Mid-Atlantic States	--	--	171	16	78	3,830	--	--	421	421	4,251	
Southern States	463	--	--	463	--	--	--	--	--	--	--	--
Total	3,358	--	171	16	78	4,293	--	--	421	421	4,251	
Sycamore												
Canada	0	968	--	7,014	669	9,865	18,517	2	--	3,727	3,729	22,246
Mid-Atlantic States	--	--	7,014	669	9,865	18,517	2	--	3,727	3,729	22,246	
Southern States	5	--	1	6	--	--	--	--	--	--	--	--
Total	974	--	7,014	670	9,865	18,523	2	--	3,727	3,729	22,246	
Tupelo												
Canada	208	1,379	--	2,609	4,445	7,482	16,122	0	--	3,908	3,908	20,030
Mid-Atlantic States	--	--	2,609	4,445	7,482	16,122	0	--	3,908	3,908	20,030	
Southern States	59	--	--	5	608	672	--	--	--	--	--	--
Total	1,439	--	2,609	4,449	8,090	16,794	0	--	3,908	3,908	20,030	
Yellow-poplar												
Canada	251	11,212	443	55,174	41,325	227,656	336,061	3	--	94,084	94,086	430,147
Mid-Atlantic States	--	--	55,174	41,325	227,656	336,061	3	--	94,084	94,086	430,147	
Southern States	701	--	101	27,549	28,351	--	--	--	--	--	--	--
Total	11,914	443	55,174	41,427	255,204	364,412	3	--	94,084	94,086	430,147	
Other hardwoods												
Canada	283	2,674	60	520	13,834	17,628	45,793	0	--	4,499	4,499	50,292
Mid-Atlantic States	--	--	520	13,834	17,628	45,793	0	--	4,499	4,499	50,292	
Southern States	--	85	10,001	10,086	--	--	--	--	--	--	--	--
Total	2,674	579	10,854	13,919	27,629	55,938	0	--	4,499	4,499	50,292	

(Table 12 continued on next page)

63

(Table 12 continued)

Product form, species group, and destination	Production by state[a]								Imports					
	Delaware	Maryland	New Jersey	New York	Ohio	Pennsyl-vania	West Virginia	Regional Total	Central States	New England States	Southern States	Canada	Total imports	Total receipts
Total hardwood roundwood														
Canada	--	--	--	102,306	--	--	--	102,306	--	--	--	--	--	--
Mid-Atlantic States	4,788	82,879	--	317,951	260,292	612,809	537,910	1,816,628	33	21,373	169,638	--	191,045	2,007,673
New England States	--	--	--	61	--	--	--	61	--	--	--	--	--	--
Southern States	--	2,416	--	--	--	2,069	166,021	170,507	--	--	--	--	--	--
Total	4,788	85,295	--	420,318	260,292	614,879	703,931	2,089,502	33	21,373	169,638	--	191,045	2,007,673
Hardwood residues														
Canada	--	--	--	607	--	--	--	607	--	--	--	--	--	--
Mid-Atlantic States	--	35,444	--	173,669	239,240	426,489	149,804	1,024,645	10,310	17,606	39,508	5,959	73,384	1,098,029
Southern States	--	15,772	--	--	350	--	234,586	250,709	--	--	--	--	--	--
Total	--	51,216	--	174,276	239,590	426,489	384,390	1,275,961	10,310	17,606	39,508	5,959	73,384	1,098,029
Total hardwood material														
Canada	--	--	--	102,913	--	--	--	102,913	--	--	--	--	--	--
Mid-Atlantic States	4,788	118,323	--	491,619	499,531	1,039,299	687,713	2,841,273	10,344	38,979	209,146	5,959	264,428	3,105,702
New England States	--	--	--	61	--	--	--	61	--	--	--	--	--	--
Southern States	--	18,188	--	--	350	2,069	400,607	421,215	--	--	--	--	--	--
Total	4,788	136,511	--	594,593	499,882	1,041,368	1,088,320	3,365,463	10,344	38,979	209,146	5,959	264,428	3,105,702
Total all roundwood														
Canada	--	--	--	111,176	--	--	--	111,176	--	--	--	--	--	--
Mid-Atlantic States	27,287	136,519	5,510	488,346	357,323	737,040	615,778	2,367,803	3,575	104,756	323,640	2,719	434,691	2,802,493
New England States	--	--	1,496	1,496	--	--	--	1,496	--	--	--	--	--	--
Southern States	--	2,569	--	--	--	2,069	169,321	173,959	--	--	--	--	--	--
Total	27,287	139,087	5,510	601,019	357,323	739,110	785,099	2,654,434	3,575	104,756	323,640	2,719	434,691	2,802,493
Total all residues														
Canada	--	--	--	607	--	--	--	607	--	--	--	--	--	--
Mid-Atlantic States	--	72,778	--	188,279	248,087	615,644	151,715	1,276,503	10,790	27,942	72,357	5,959	117,048	1,393,552
Southern States	--	62,529	--	--	350	--	239,822	302,701	--	--	--	--	--	--
Total	--	135,307	--	188,886	248,438	615,644	391,537	1,579,812	10,790	27,942	72,357	5,959	117,048	1,393,552
Total all wood material														
Canada	--	--	--	111,784	--	--	--	111,784	--	--	--	--	--	--
Mid-Atlantic States	27,287	209,297	5,510	676,625	605,410	1,352,684	767,493	3,644,306	14,366	132,698	395,997	8,678	551,739	4,196,045
New England States	--	--	1,496	1,496	--	--	--	1,496	--	--	--	--	--	--
Southern States	--	65,098	--	--	350	2,069	409,143	476,660	--	--	--	--	--	--
Total	27,287	274,394	5,510	789,904	605,760	1,354,754	1,176,636	4,234,246	14,366	132,698	395,997	8,678	551,739	4,196,045

[a] Vertical columns of figures under the box heading "Production by State" present the amount of roundwood cut or residue generated in each state

All table cells without observations are indicated by --. Table value of 0 indicates the volume rounds to less than 1 standard cord, unpeeled. Columns and rows may not add to their totals due to rounding.

Table 13.—Mid-Atlantic States pulpwood production in thousand standard cords, unpeeled, from roundwood by state and species group, 2001-2006[a]

State	All species			Hemlock		Pine		
	2001	2005	2006	2005	2006	2001	2005	2006
Delaware	0	23	27	--	--	--	22	22
Maryland	176	130	139	0	0	--	41	53
New Jersey	17	4	6	--	--	--	3	6
New York	429	628	601	52	79	--	126	68
Ohio	330	347	357	4	4	--	87	93
Pennsylvania	633	715	739	53	50	--	72	68
West Virginia	732	712	785	3	4	--	83	76
Total Mid-Atlantic States	1,938	2,559	2,654	113	138	--	434	387

State	Other softwoods			Birch			Maple		
	2001[b]	2005	2006	2001	2005	2006	2001	2005	2006
Delaware	0	--	--	--	--	--	--	1	2
Maryland	86	0	0	--	1	1	--	18	19
New Jersey	17	0	0	--	--	--	--	0	--
New York	204	25	33	--	69	65	--	203	197
Ohio	50	--	--	--	0	1	--	49	50
Pennsylvania	146	6	6	--	33	33	--	184	199
West Virginia	92	1	1	--	21	24	--	121	140
Total Mid-Atlantic States	594	32	40	--	124	123	--	576	605

State	Oak			Yellow-poplar			Other hardwoods		
	2001	2005	2006	2001	2005	2006	2001[c]	2005	2006
Delaware	--	1	1	--	0	0	0	0	1
Maryland	--	29	28	--	12	12	90	28	26
New Jersey	--	0	--	--	0	--	1	0	--
New York	--	27	30	--	0	0	226	125	129
Ohio	--	60	58	--	53	55	280	94	96
Pennsylvania	--	137	146	--	43	41	486	186	195
West Virginia	--	104	115	--	209	255	640	169	170
Total Mid-Atlantic States	--	358	377	--	318	364	1,723	604	620

[a] Data is not available for 2002, 2003, and 2004.
[b] Includes all softwoods in 2001.
[c] Includes all hardwoods in 2001.
All table cells without observations are indicated by – . Table value of 0 indicates the volume rounds to less than 1,000 standard cords, unpeeled. Columns and rows may not add to their totals due to rounding.

Table 14.—Pulpwood production in standard cords, unpeeled, by mill type, product form, state of origin, and species group, Mid-Atlantic States, 2006

Product form and species group	State of origin for pulp mills								Mills					
	All States	Delaware	Mary-land	New Jersey	New York	Ohio	Pennsyl-vania	West Virginia	All States	Mary-land	New York	Ohio	Pennsyl-vania	West Virginia
Softwood roundwood														
Balsam fir	9,749	--	--	--	9,749	--	--	--	58	--	58	--	--	--
Hemlock	137,644	--	332	--	79,178	4,071	50,329	3,734	556	--	237	243	76	--
Shortleaf/loblolly pine	56,201	19,881	31,362	19	--	1,502	358	3,079	448	--	--	148	--	300
Red pine	9,092	--	582	--	1,580	2,332	4,583	15	1,879	--	--	1,601	213	65
White pine	146,125	--	1,847	16	59,165	33,906	36,709	14,482	26,868	15	7,008	11,689	1,754	6,402
O her pines	129,983	2,618	19,471	5,475	442	36,869	23,397	41,711	16,015	32	136	4,669	871	10,307
Spruce	29,777	--	150	1	22,900	--	5,655	1,071	247	--	247	--	--	--
Tamarack	285	--	--	--	--	--	285	--	--	--	--	--	--	--
Total softwood roundwood	518,856	22,499	53,744	5,511	173,014	78,680	121,316	64,092	46,071	47	7,686	18,350	2,914	17,074
Hardwood roundwood														
Ash	65,664	18	1,638	--	28,977	10,933	15,028	9,070	18,349	--	4,692	1,648	12,009	--
Aspen/balsam poplar	28,875	11	192	--	17,533	4,094	6,053	992	15,809	9	2,558	3,817	5,856	3,569
Basswood	25,992	--	2,540	--	1,049	2,573	6,705	13,125	41,262	563	1,981	1,426	6,392	30,900
Beech	79,618	64	1,349	--	50,434	7,034	9,985	10,752	27,636	--	2,207	923	12,014	12,492
White birch	25,051	--	--	--	24,906	--	145	--	886	--	102	--	784	--
Yellow birch	45,703	--	216	--	37,975	32	2,371	5,109	2,856	--	544	--	2,312	--
O her birch	23,687	--	826	--	170	337	14,597	7,757	25,262	165	906	130	12,845	11,216
Black cherry	105,665	42	7,105	--	15,641	10,924	52,909	19,044	38,326	--	2,800	2,622	32,904	--
Black walnut	2,456	--	89	--	--	1,496	789	82	234	--	--	--	234	--
Cottonwood	1,429	--	127	--	--	1,124	178	--	227	--	--	227	--	--
Elm	9,322	9	565	--	261	4,426	2,052	2,009	9,125	291	83	3,663	1,496	3,592
Hickory	48,593	12	2,804	--	--	19,289	8,026	18,462	3,403	--	--	--	3,403	--
Hard maple	174,591	--	3,801	--	105,759	18,200	24,766	22,065	34,675	--	8,007	--	26,668	--
Soft maple	222,960	1,735	13,424	--	72,568	19,685	76,417	39,131	173,878	1,397	10,432	12,164	71,192	78,693
Red oak group	148,040	850	13,473	--	18,832	22,195	45,096	47,594	34,144	--	3,880	--	30,264	--
White oak group	164,349	633	14,362	--	6,097	35,508	40,339	67,410	30,660	--	898	--	29,762	--
Sweetgum	4,169	670	3,358	--	--	126	15	--	124	--	--	45	1	78
Sycamore	6,564	0	754	--	--	3,711	187	1,912	11,960	220	--	3,304	483	7,953
Tupelo/gum	8,522	208	1,330	--	--	1,662	2,660	2,662	8,272	108	--	947	1,789	5,428
Yellow-poplar	101,125	251	8,267	--	87	26,797	16,716	49,007	263,280	3,646	356	28,376	24,705	206,197
O her hardwoods	39,934	283	2,674	--	124	8,335	11,917	16,601	15,961	--	456	2,519	1,958	11,028
Total hardwood roundwood	1,332,309	4,786	78,894	0	380,413	198,481	336,951	332,784	756,329	6,399	39,902	61,811	277,071	371,146
Total Roundwood	1,851,165	27,285	132,638	5,511	553,427	277,161	458,267	396,876	802,400	6,446	47,588	80,161	279,985	388,220
Residues														
Softwood	294,872	--	84,091	--	11,974	3,384	188,276	7,147	8,977	--	2,636	5,463	878	--
Hardwood	770,247	--	51,216	--	26,017	214,131	133,487	345,396	495,747	--	148,258	25,459	293,003	29,027
Total residues	1,065,119	--	135,307	--	37,991	217,515	321,763	352,543	504,724	--	150,894	30,922	293,881	29,027
State total	2,916,284	27,285	267,945	5,511	591,418	494,676	780,030	749,419	1,307,124	6,446	198,482	111,083	573,866	417,247

All table cells without observations are indicated by --. Table value of 0 indicates the volume rounds to less than 1 standard cord, unpeeled. Columns and rows may not add to their totals due to rounding.

66

Table 15.—Pulpwood production in standard cords, unpeeled, by mill type, product form, species group, and percent change, Mid-Atlantic States, 2005 and 2006

Product form and species group	Pulp mills			Composite mills		
	2005	2006	Percent change	2005	2006	Percent change
Softwood roundwood						
Balsam fir	6,508	9,749	50%	58	58	0%
Hemlock	112,929	137,644	22%	242	556	130%
Shortleaf/loblolly pine	47,752	56,201	18%	472	448	-5%
Red pine	14,626	9,092	-38%	1,672	1,879	12%
White pine	197,772	146,125	-26%	27,844	26,868	-4%
Other pine	126,375	129,983	3%	17,351	16,015	-8%
Spruce	25,196	29,777	18%	247	247	0%
Tamarack	317	285	-10%	--	--	--
Total softwood roundwood	531,475	518,856	-2%	47,886	46,071	-4%
Hardwood roundwood						
Ash	66,195	65,664	-1%	20,528	18,349	-11%
Aspen/balsam poplar	23,273	28,875	24%	9,452	15,809	67%
Basswood	22,908	25,992	13%	37,524	41,262	10%
Beech	79,592	79,618	0%	24,638	27,636	12%
White birch	25,248	25,051	-1%	882	886	0%
Yellow birch	49,450	45,703	-8%	3,297	2,856	-13%
Other birch	22,792	23,687	4%	22,814	25,262	11%
Black cherry	102,798	105,665	3%	33133	38326	16%
Black walnut	2,356	2,456	4%	229	234	2%
Cottonwood	1,752	1,429	-18%	187	227	21%
Elm	9,969	9,322	-6%	1,331	9,125	586%
Hickory	46,196	48,593	5%	3,005	3,403	13%
Hard maple	216,725	174,591	-19%	28,498	34,675	22%
Soft maple	173,618	222,960	28%	157,425	173,878	10%
Red oak group	143,227	148,040	3%	30,597	34,144	12%
White oak group	155,824	164,349	5%	28,460	30,660	8%
Sweetgum	4,313	4,169	-3%	44	124	182%
Sycamore	6,966	6,564	-6%	12,200	11,960	-2%
Tupelo/gum	8,662	8,522	-2%	7,500	8,272	10%
Yellow-poplar	91,489	101,125	11%	226,244	263,280	16%
Other hardwoods	38,490	39,934	4%	40,169	15,961	-60%
Total hardwood roundwood	1,291,843	1,332,309	3%	688,158	756,329	10%
Total Roundwood	1,823,318	1,851,165	2%	736,044	802,400	9%
Residues	0					
Softwood	299,162	294,872	-1%	7,740	8,977	16%
Hardwood	796,079	770,247	-3%	420,605	495,747	18%
Total residues	1,095,241	1,065,119	-3%	428,345	504,724	18%
State total	2,918,559	2,916,284	0%	1,164,389	1,307,124	12%

All table cells without observations are indicated by --. Table value of 0 indicates the volume rounds to less than 1 standard cord, unpeeled. Columns and rows may not add to their totals due to rounding.

Table 16.—Pulpwood production in standard cords, unpeeled, from roundwood by state, Forest Inventory Unit, county, and species group, Delaware, Maryland, and New Jersey, 2006

Forest Inventory Unit and county[a]	All species	Hemlock	Shortleaf/ loblolly pine	Red pine	White pine	Other pines	Spruce	Ash	Aspen/ balsam poplar	Bass- wood	Beech	Yellow birch	Other birch
DELAWARE													
Kent	3,804	--	1,497	--	--	1,540	--	16	--	--	11	--	--
Sussex	23,483	--	18,384	--	--	1,078	--	3	11	--	53	--	--
State total	27,287	--	19,881	--	--	2,618	--	18	11	--	64	--	--
MARYLAND													
North Central													
Anne Arundel	3,705	--	74	--	45	597	--	--	6	--	63	--	20
Baltimore	2,376	156	--	--	--	595	--	13	26	--	28	--	--
Caroline	1,501	--	292	--	--	320	--	1	--	--	0	--	1
Carroll	267	--	--	--	61	--	--	6	--	--	0	--	7
Cecil	3,248	--	17	--	--	556	--	14	65	--	92	--	20
Frederick	2,223	--	--	--	--	492	--	83	--	--	13	--	13
Harford	1,831	25	1	--	--	130	--	23	4	--	49	--	90
Howard	1,297	--	117	--	21	135	--	60	--	--	0	--	--
Kent	27	--	27	--	--	--	--	--	--	--	--	--	--
Montgomery	1,270	--	--	--	--	108	14	38	--	--	81	--	--
Prince George's	4,982	--	20	--	--	1,056	--	82	--	--	163	5	37
Queen Anne's	45	--	45	--	--	--	--	--	--	--	--	--	--
Talbot	618	--	202	--	--	22	--	--	13	--	3	--	--
Washington	402	1	--	--	7	1	--	15	--	3	4	--	10
Total	23,792	183	796	--	134	4,012	14	334	113	3	497	5	199

Southern											
Calvert	157	--	32	--	58	--	--	3	--	8	--	--
Charles	13,966	--	2,899	--	9,073	--	--	82	--	77	21	2
St. Mary's	14,574	--	6,078	--	2,679	37	11	11	37	452	12	21
Total	28,696	--	9,009	--	11,810	37	11	96	37	537	32	22
Lower Eastern Shore											
Dorchester	2,919	--	11	--	1,765	11	--	--	19	4	--	--
Somerset	15,410	--	--	--	15,189	--	16	--	--	1	--	--
Wicomico	5,288	--	--	--	4,364	--	7	--	90	24	--	--
Worcester	699	--	--	--	238	--	11	--	10	6	--	--
Total	24,316	--	11	--	21,557	11	35	--	118	35	--	--
Western											
Allegany	15,415	82	1,674	--	3,542	--	127	7	667	5	--	221
Garrett	46,868	67	43	582	21	136	1,047	43	2,434	275	179	549
Total	62,283	149	1,718	582	3,563	136	1,174	50	3,100	280	179	770
State total	139,087	332	1,863	582	19,503	150	1,638	200	3,103	1,349	216	991

NEW JERSEY

Burlington	132	10	12	--	110	--	--	--	--	--	--	--
Camden	4,954	--	--	--	4,954	--	--	--	--	--	--	--
Cape May	88	--	--	--	88	--	--	--	--	--	--	--
Cumberland	47	--	--	--	47	--	--	--	--	--	--	--
Gloucester	9	0	1	--	8	--	--	--	--	--	--	--
Monmouth	51	9	--	--	42	--	--	--	--	--	--	--
Ocean	229	--	3	--	225	--	--	--	--	--	--	--
State total	5,510	19	16	--	5,475	--	--	--	--	--	--	--

(Table 16 continued on next page)

(Table 16 continued)

Forest Inventory Unit and county[a]	Black cherry	Black walnut	Cotton-wood	Elm	Hickory	Hard maple	Soft maple	Species group Red oak group	White oak group	Sweet-gum	Syca-more	Tupelo/ gum	Yellow-poplar	Other hard-woods
DELAWARE														
Kent	26	--	--	9	4	--	167	136	118	112	--	65	87	14
Sussex	16	--	--	--	8	--	1,568	713	515	558	0	143	164	268
State total	42	--	--	9	12	--	1,735	850	633	670	0	208	251	283
MARYLAND														
North Central														
Anne Arundel	149	2	--	--	124	--	207	413	226	753	16	124	683	202
Baltimore	34	18	--	5	86	1	137	385	112	--	60	12	685	23
Caroline	13	--	--	--	16	--	265	168	70	201	7	37	79	32
Carroll	14	1	--	--	15	--	9	58	40	--	--	3	49	3
Cecil	94	22	--	--	129	--	315	555	171	273	102	4	595	225
Frederick	16	4	--	5	57	13	163	177	262	--	27	28	826	44
Harford	124	10	--	25	33	--	132	142	192	117	13	17	671	32
Howard	39	5	--	--	76	--	321	240	88	--	24	14	154	5
Kent	--	--	--	--	--	--	--	--	--	--	--	--	--	--
Montgomery	52	0	127	17	12	--	141	201	82	--	64	10	229	94
Prince George's	33	22	--	41	198	--	429	670	591	317	96	274	888	59
Queen Anne's	--	--	--	--	--	--	--	--	--	--	--	--	--	--
Ta bot	1	--	--	2	14	--	33	109	7	68	36	26	4	80
Washington	2	3	--	0	10	7	22	42	58	--	16	1	199	0
Total	572	88	127	96	769	22	2,174	3,159	1,898	1,729	459	549	5,061	800

Southern

Calvert	0	--	0	3	--	5	8	12	5	2	2	18	0
Charles	22	2	17	80	--	149	288	335	351	15	45	475	34
St. Mary's	8	--	--	137	--	688	923	781	730	12	153	1,832	20
Total	30	2	18	219	--	842	1,219	1,128	1,086	29	201	2,325	54

Lower Eastern Shore

Dorchester	11	--	--	30	--	329	281	127	202	--	54	58	27
Somerset	1	--	--	--	--	86	2	16	70	6	15	--	7
Wicomico	3	--	--	1	--	238	69	47	176	--	92	98	78
Worcester	2	--	--	1	--	195	17	36	95	--	31	25	32
Total	17	--	--	33	--	849	369	226	543	6	193	181	144

Western

Allegany	174	--	613	342	968	540	982	2,952	--	457	193	1,450	420
Garrett	6,312	--	130	1,442	2,812	10,415	7,746	8,157	--	23	303	2,897	1,255
Total	6,486	127	743	1,783	3,780	10,955	8,727	11,109	--	480	496	4,347	1,676
State total	7,105	89	856	2,804	3,801	14,820	13,473	14,362	3,358	974	1,439	11,914	2,674

NEW JERSEY

Burlington	--	--	--	--	--	--	--	--	--	--	--	--	--
Camden	--	--	--	--	--	--	--	--	--	--	--	--	--
Cape May	--	--	--	--	--	--	--	--	--	--	--	--	--
Cumberland	--	--	--	--	--	--	--	--	--	--	--	--	--
Gloucester	--	--	--	--	--	--	--	--	--	--	--	--	--
Monmouth	--	--	--	--	--	--	--	--	--	--	--	--	--
Ocean	--	--	--	--	--	--	--	--	--	--	--	--	--
State total	--	--	--	--	--	--	--	--	--	--	--	--	--

[a] Includes only those counties that supplied pulpwood in 2006.

All table cells without observations are indicated by -- . Table value of 0 indicates the volume rounds to less than 1 standard cord, unpeeled.

Columns and rows may not add to their totals due to rounding.

Table 17.—Pulpwood production in standard cords, unpeeled, from roundwood by Forest Inventory Unit, county, and species group, New York, 2006

Forest Inventory Unit and county[a]	All species	Balsam fir	Hemlock	Red pine	White pine	Other pine	Spruce	Ash	Aspen/ balsam poplar	Basswood	Beech
Adirondack											
Clinton	23,195	463	1,168	2	4,510	0	115	2,003	828	146	2,582
Franklin	79,054	654	997	–	3,065	–	1,639	3,842	2,660	218	12,907
Jefferson	4,927	–	145	–	368	–	84	1,026	125	–	630
St. Lawrence	58,093	579	1,347	–	9,882	136	1,373	3,375	1,792	–	8,230
Total	165,269	1,695	3,657	2	17,825	136	3,210	10,246	5,404	365	24,349
Lake Plain											
Erie	323	–	–	–	–	–	–	–	–	–	41
Madison	75	1	5	–	34	–	10	2	0	–	6
Monroe	12	–	–	–	12	–	–	–	–	–	–
Onondaga	808	–	119	–	689	–	–	–	–	–	–
Ontario	179	–	–	107	71	1	–	–	–	–	–
Oswego	4,391	–	3,303	–	15	–	118	114	33	–	–
Yates	28	–	9	–	0	–	–	1	3	1	–
Total	5,817	1	3,435	107	823	1	128	116	51	1	47
Western Adirondack											
Fulton	17,835	130	5,385	–	2,608	–	596	1,132	535	–	93
Herkimer	23,660	252	1,232	–	209	–	2,028	1,219	613	–	4,012
Lewis	26,668	1,625	2,236	154	893	8	2,869	1,388	775	–	1,088
Onieda	16,413	131	1,883	29	1,222	56	476	892	372	12	2,342
Total	84,576	2,137	10,736	183	4,932	64	5,969	4,631	2,295	12	7,536
Eastern Adirondack											
Essex	93,793	1,198	8,242	13	7,701	7	3,877	5,991	3,715	556	8,149
Hamilton	42,632	1,924	835	–	2,820	–	3,080	2,147	850	–	5,705
Warren	49,968	2,353	14,997	–	10,292	–	1,252	1,429	1,366	–	976
Total	186,392	5,475	24,074	13	20,812	7	8,209	9,568	5,930	556	14,829
Southwest Highlands											
Allegany	3,794	–	176	474	246	234	190	186	143	148	296
Cattaraugus	5,455	–	810	276	406	52	–	505	124	101	288
Chautauqua	181	–	–	16	–	–	–	22	31	6	15
Steuben	7,562	–	310	16	462	61	–	1,296	454	205	392
Total	16,992	–	1,297	766	1,114	347	190	2,009	753	460	992

South-Central Highlands

County											
Broome	7,164	--	875	191	493	437	--	670	301	266	127
Chemung	3,307	--	173	--	156	--	2	343	264	442	178
Chenango	6,553	--	41	4	38	--	--	456	243	288	413
Cortland	6,159	--	635	134	2,122	--	--	556	77	70	71
Delaware	5,006	--	2,929	15	751	176	--	130	21	22	54
Otsego	3,263	2	530	73	300	89	5	219	82	11	390
Schuyler	2,354	--	149	--	497	171	--	244	135	152	31
Tioga	2,471	--	87	75	82	--	8	245	300	103	7
Tompkins	3,037	--	9	--	30	--	0	330	330	252	144
Total	**39,314**	**2**	**5,427**	**492**	**4,468**	**873**	**16**	**3,192**	**1,753**	**1,606**	**1,415**
Capitol District											
Albany	2,347	--	987	11	789	7	6	31	71	--	51
Columbia	555	--	46	--	--	--	--	61	12	--	--
Montgomery	1,544	--	884	--	--	--	--	104	43	--	--
Rensselaer	16,196	353	5,174	--	1,555	1,102	--	586	153	--	356
Saratoga	56,142	137	13,793	--	10,560	3,092	--	1,707	2,498	--	2,188
Washington	22,226	--	8,432	7	3,126	333	--	1,178	1,044	--	767
Total	**99,012**	**490**	**29,316**	**18**	**16,030**	**4,534**	**6**	**3,667**	**3,821**	**--**	**3,362**
Catskill-Lower Hudson											
Dutchess	82	--	11	--	--	6	--	10	1	--	--
Greene	1,337	1	784	--	35	1	--	65	30	7	23
Orange	6	--	2	--	--	1	--	0	--	--	--
Schoharie	1,025	6	538	--	12	24	--	64	28	17	28
Suffolk	26	--	--	--	26	--	--	--	--	--	--
Sullivan	394	--	72	--	25	5	--	29	2	--	24
Ulster	777	--	66	--	71	--	--	71	22	6	38
Total	**3,646**	**8**	**1,473**	**--**	**169**	**35**	**--**	**240**	**84**	**29**	**112**
Grand Total	**601,019**	**9,808**	**79,415**	**1,580**	**66,173**	**23,147**	**578**	**33,670**	**20,091**	**3,030**	**52,641**

(Table 17 continued on next page)

(Table 17 continued)

Forest Inventory Unit and county[a]	Species group										
	White birch	Yellow birch	Other birch	Black cherry	Elm	Hard maple	Soft maple	Red oak group	White oak group	Yellow-poplar	Other hard-woods
Adirondack											
Clinton	1,340	1,515	66	534	125	3,944	3,042	425	326	--	60
Franklin	4,789	8,815	68	2,571	98	18,509	15,065	1,570	1,587	--	--
Jefferson	207	297	2	84	--	1,204	587	87	82	--	--
St. Lawrence	2,793	4,298	4	1,927	--	11,887	8,171	1,158	1,142	--	--
Total	9,130	14,925	141	5,116	223	35,544	26,865	3,240	3,137	--	60
Lake Plain											
Erie	--	--	--	120	--	97	49	--	--	--	--
Madison	2	3	--	1	--	4	4	1	1	--	--
Monroe	--	--	--	--	--	--	--	--	--	--	--
Onondaga	--	--	--	--	--	--	--	--	--	--	--
Ontario	--	--	--	--	--	--	--	--	--	--	--
Oswego	--	40	--	200	--	128	426	15	--	--	--
Yates	--	1	--	1	--	4	3	4	--	--	--
Total	2	44	--	323	--	233	483	20	1	--	--
Western Adirondack											
Fulton	217	1,088	--	1,080	--	1,562	3,284	110	15	--	--
Herkimer	1,072	2,276	--	805	--	5,262	3,799	439	442	--	--
Lewis	307	1,656	0	1,969	--	6,293	5,119	165	124	--	--
Oneida	931	1,429	1	649	6	2,154	2,773	397	383	275	--
Total	2,527	6,449	2	4,503	6	15,270	14,974	1,111	965	275	--
Eastern Adirondack											
Essex	7,093	7,678	8	1,127	24	24,517	8,204	5,034	660	--	--
Hamilton	1,422	3,577	--	718	--	13,203	5,418	453	481	--	--
Warren	2,098	1,443	--	470	--	6,461	4,410	2,260	160	--	--
Total	10,613	12,697	8	2,314	24	44,181	18,032	7,748	1,301	--	--
Southwest Highlands											
Allegany	--	25	75	146	3	601	558	245	39	--	9
Cattaraugus	--	54	17	643	7	837	919	202	74	87	52
Chautauqua	--	2	--	23	4	25	46	2	0	0	4
Steuben	31	17	141	212	12	1,068	1,572	1,021	278	--	12
Total	31	98	233	1,023	25	2,531	3,095	1,470	392	87	76

South-Central Highlands

County											
Broome	--	39	98	320	1	440	1,893	881	--	96	36
Chemung	2	10	86	6	--	530	649	445	--	21	--
Chenango	--	240	150	570	10	1,433	2,295	215	--	90	68
Cortland	--	87	96	436	40	1,159	568	--	--	--	107
Delaware	13	42	10	68	2	273	441	51	--	6	2
Otsego	158	227	5	85	0	379	488	151	--	69	--
Schuyler	57	23	5	123	4	394	249	94	--	14	11
Tioga	1	2	19	122	--	406	515	338	--	151	10
Tompkins	--	23	153	295	3	458	182	438	79	104	207
Total	231	696	621	2,025	61	5,471	7,279	2,612	79	551	442

Capitol District

County											
Albany	34	35	--	34	--	123	95	65	--	8	--
Columbia	17	4	--	48	--	129	114	123	--	--	--
Montgomery	--	3	--	49	--	247	158	56	--	--	--
Rensselaer	365	545	--	529	--	1,480	2,969	971	--	59	--
Saratoga	1,292	2,353	--	1,713	--	5,604	6,893	3,949	--	361	--
Washington	737	577	--	733	--	2,497	1,621	1,049	--	125	--
Total	2,445	3,518	--	3,106	--	10,080	11,851	6,213	--	554	--

Catskill-Lower Hudson

County											
Dutchess	--	0	--	8	--	10	17	19	--	--	--
Greene	13	43	10	13	0	148	62	83	--	19	--
Orange	11	--	--	--	--	1	1	2	--	--	--
Schoharie	--	9	2	5	--	138	69	69	--	6	--
Suffolk	--	--	--	--	--	--	--	--	--	0	--
Sullivan	--	10	26	--	3	27	104	30	--	36	0
Ulster	4	29	33	5	2	131	167	94	--	35	1
Total	28	91	72	31	5	455	421	297	--	95	1
Grand Total	25,008	38,519	1,077	18,441	344	113,766	83,000	22,712	443	6,995	579

[a] Includes only those counties that supplied pulpwood in 2006.
All table cells without observations are indicated by --. Table value of 0 indicates the volume rounds to less than 1 standard cord, unpeeled.
Columns and rows may not add to their totals due to rounding.

Table 18.—Pulpwood production in standard cords, unpeeled, from roundwood by Forest Inventory Unit, county, and species group, Ohio, 2006

Forest Inventory Unit and county[a]	All species	Hemlock	Shortleaf/ loblolly pine	Red pine	White pine	Other pine	Ash	Aspen/ balsam poplar	Bass-wood	Beech	Yellow birch	Other birch	Black cherry
South-Central													
Adams	3,015	--	--	--	--	789	220	--	64	139	--	--	28
Gallia	15,567	--	102	317	622	1,433	461	248	--	428	--	141	236
Highland	1,695	--	--	--	23	--	228	--	89	89	--	--	45
Jackson	54,128	2,316	1,023	--	10,425	4,775	1,469	1,002	8	172	--	--	887
Lawrence	8,316	--	--	501	153	766	67	165	55	815	--	--	24
Pike	31,972	--	--	--	1,455	4,437	370	348	1,062	745	--	--	845
Ross	23,986	--	--	--	4,576	1,354	1,317	--	100	333	--	--	899
Scioto	8,900	--	86	--	411	543	98	20	46	72	--	--	241
Total	147,580	2,316	1,211	818	17,667	14,095	4,230	1,783	1,334	2,792	--	141	3,206
Southeastern													
Athens	6,977	--	--	--	416	128	331	411	140	172	--	--	51
Hocking	20,495	1,746	--	--	3,658	2,813	167	264	7	720	--	116	503
Meigs	13,933	--	20	--	816	1,956	224	456	27	167	--	17	35
Morgan	8,656	--	--	242	3,603	--	296	120	22	65	9	--	70
Perry	5,315	--	--	--	--	374	73	795	23	110	--	1	301
Vinton	44,553	--	290	--	61	12,801	448	682	400	1,446	--	--	758
Washington	6,321	--	128	--	--	1,799	116	174	10	235	--	--	74
Total	106,250	1,746	438	242	8,553	19,871	1,654	2,902	629	2,914	9	134	1,793
East-Central													
Belmont	7,273	--	--	--	--	1,819	382	28	92	184	--	--	853
Carroll	10,214	--	--	--	5,707	2,224	208	--	--	14	--	--	416
Coshocton	7,716	--	--	--	386	1,608	204	272	430	371	--	37	292
Guernsey	5,510	--	--	85	1,882	128	162	500	7	193	--	--	472
Harrison	5,451	--	--	630	2,462	--	105	133	--	19	--	--	430
Holmes	2,510	--	--	--	197	--	703	67	44	19	--	--	396
Jefferson	2,457	--	--	--	--	--	48	84	55	14	--	--	1,074
Monroe	6,021	--	--	--	626	171	169	--	61	40	--	--	362
Muskingum	6,817	--	--	--	1,160	78	262	647	22	135	--	--	290
Noble	4,732	--	--	414	1,726	62	217	230	97	2	--	--	224
Tuscarawas	3,803	--	--	29	1,078	--	36	154	--	55	--	3	189
Total	62,505	--	--	1,158	15,224	6,089	2,495	2,115	809	1,045	--	39	4,996
Northeastern													
Ashland	3,648	86	--	333	641	--	408	94	65	29	--	--	339
Columbiana	2,708	21	--	--	265	12	95	131	116	3	--	23	285
Cuyahoga	898	--	--	--	--	--	79	--	102	59	--	--	61

County													
Erie	105	--	--	--	--	--	12	--	--	--	--	--	--
Geauga	1,676	--	--	--	143	104	47	161	22	--	--	--	292
Huron	544	--	--	--	133	--	15	12	--	--	--	--	36
Lorain	1,214	--	--	--	212	--	112	19	19	--	--	--	14
Mahoning	965	--	--	--	19	12	--	19	--	--	--	--	87
Medina	2,240	--	--	449	547	--	75	155	--	15	--	--	111
Portage	1,941	--	--	114	194	199	54	64	1	--	--	--	426
Richland	1,891	--	1,013	--	212	28	--	25	--	--	--	--	88
Stark	1,189	--	--	--	42	289	86	46	--	--	--	--	213
Summit	954	--	--	--	70	9	--	125	--	--	--	--	171
Trumbull	2,065	--	--	--	50	108	10	19	--	60	--	--	261
Wayne	1,592	145	--	--	57	--	174	174	--	--	23	16	139
Total	**23,631**	**252**	**--**	**1,345**	**1,469**	**87**	**975**	**683**	**909**	**--**	**23**	**62**	**2,524**
Southwestern													
Clark	388	--	--	--	87	--	--	--	--	0	--	--	90
Fairfield	1,794	--	--	--	118	1	--	92	--	92	--	92	174
Fayette	135	--	--	--	38	26	--	--	--	--	--	--	--
Franklin	368	--	--	--	28	--	--	5	--	--	--	--	--
Greene	433	--	--	--	64	--	--	--	--	--	--	--	65
Licking	2,966	--	--	875	91	57	78	78	0	--	--	--	165
Madison	274	--	--	--	58	--	--	--	--	--	--	--	31
Pickaway	532	--	--	--	76	--	--	--	--	--	--	--	11
Total	**6,890**	**--**	**--**	**875**	**559**	**85**	**78**	**97**	**--**	**--**	**--**	**92**	**537**
Northwestern													
Champaign	466	--	--	--	183	--	--	--	--	--	--	--	45
Crawford	342	--	--	--	49	--	7	59	--	--	--	--	--
Delaware	145	--	--	--	32	--	--	--	--	--	--	--	12
Hancock	954	--	--	--	264	--	50	56	--	--	--	--	--
Hardin	283	--	--	--	20	--	140	--	--	--	--	--	--
Knox	3,287	--	--	1,743	206	52	--	--	--	--	--	--	354
Logan	606	--	--	--	136	--	13	27	--	--	--	--	37
Marion	272	--	--	--	--	--	16	--	--	--	--	--	--
Morrow	1,324	--	7	--	319	--	43	52	--	--	--	--	33
Sandusky	167	--	--	--	70	--	63	--	--	--	--	--	--
Seneca	365	--	--	--	84	--	37	4	--	--	--	--	2
Union	54	--	--	--	7	--	--	--	--	--	--	--	--
Williams	684	--	--	364	--	--	75	--	--	--	--	--	--
Wood	1,396	--	--	--	--	1,396	--	--	--	--	--	--	--
Wyandot	121	--	--	--	--	--	23	1	--	--	--	--	7
Total	**10,466**	**--**	**370**	**1,808**	**1,369**	**52**	**466**	**199**	**--**	**--**	**--**	**--**	**490**
State total	**357,323**	**4,314**	**3,934**	**45,596**	**41,538**	**7,910**	**12,581**	**3,998**	**7,956**	**52**	**32**	**467**	**13,546**

(Table 18 continued on next page)

(Table 18 continued)

Forest Inventory Unit and county[a]	Species group												
	Black walnut	Cotton-wood	Elm	Hickory	Hard maple	Soft maple	Red oak group	White oak group	Sweet-gum	Syca-more	Tupelo/gum	Yellow-poplar	Other hard-woods
South-Central													
Adams	--	--	43	209	221	157	241	360	--	37	17	373	118
Gallia	--	--	437	1,626	1,164	1,884	1,483	1,036	--	237	114	2,467	1,134
Highland	--	--	60	163	145	56	158	234	--	214	13	196	70
Jackson	9	--	935	4,818	1,031	4,537	3,240	6,530	--	873	245	8,383	1,451
Lawrence	--	--	57	93	127	601	221	595	27	446	165	3,463	477
Pike	--	--	270	2,292	4,203	4,254	2,126	3,459	--	183	142	4,980	301
Ross	88	380	229	2,007	2,942	960	1,182	3,143	--	471	192	2,587	1,228
Scioto	--	--	23	630	306	750	1,247	2,529	48	156	82	1,493	119
Total	97	380	2,054	11,837	10,138	13,199	9,897	17,886	75	2,617	968	23,941	4,899
Southeastern													
Athens	18	--	558	280	308	495	244	418	--	367	72	2,338	230
Hocking	27	27	148	948	976	1,596	1,720	2,532	10	341	19	1,706	452
Meigs	40	8	117	778	404	1,308	383	880	--	1,083	176	3,686	1,354
Morgan	43	27	487	227	413	754	113	81	--	81	64	1,796	143
Perry	27	0	421	73	187	496	155	124	2	53	39	1,925	138
Vinton	6	--	136	1,833	1,812	2,369	4,810	9,943	68	271	611	5,380	427
Washington	76	--	106	227	427	315	538	748	--	50	27	1,077	195
Total	236	63	1,972	4,366	4,526	7,333	7,962	14,726	80	2,246	1,007	17,908	2,939
East-Central													
Belmont	13	39	931	71	210	655	125	79	--	66	1	1,589	136
Carroll	--	--	25	88	31	519	233	177	--	--	79	371	124
Coshocton	10	41	190	148	95	1,097	147	71	14	85	48	1,886	285
Guernsey	64	--	119	140	39	359	191	290	--	2	51	706	121
Harrison	42	7	281	112	43	241	113	37	--	1	29	657	112
Holmes	31	--	69	111	69	149	77	120	--	13	102	131	212
Jefferson	3	--	180	17	45	494	123	39	--	76	20	145	39
Monroe	46	--	158	185	216	496	323	127	--	205	12	2,525	300
Muskingum	94	--	416	167	115	624	200	47	--	911	51	1,513	83
Noble	20	26	182	120	184	228	147	338	--	8	2	413	93
Tuscarawas	26	155	68	85	58	592	97	116	2	9	31	901	118
Total	350	269	2,618	1,244	1,105	5,453	1,777	1,440	16	1,376	427	10,837	1,623
Northeastern													
Ashland	52	--	218	154	354	355	234	88	--	--	12	--	184
Columbiana	35	--	49	38	119	563	179	8	--	--	91	500	173
Cuyahoga	--	47	54	82	71	77	107	63	--	--	--	63	34

County												
Erie	28	9	--	--	--	26	23	--	--	--	--	7
Geauga	38	--	64	134	170	399	43	3	--	--	2	30
Huron	13	15	4	54	1	115	76	69	--	--	--	--
Lorain	7	54	35	50	23	488	114	71	7	--	--	8
Mahoning	--	--	48	36	42	375	138	179	--	--	1	8
Medina	24	163	25	31	133	239	41	57	--	--	176	--
Portage	--	--	59	72	66	338	46	53	82	39	79	55
Richland	19	--	92	24	230	69	28	--	--	8	--	57
Stark	9	--	83	63	3	169	16	39	3	5	35	88
Summit	--	7	27	10	31	90	136	37	29	11	192	9
Trumbull	--	17	98	160	7	753	378	17	--	6	17	80
Wayne	12	--	16	36	5	346	63	31	154	--	366	32
Total	**236**	**313**	**872**	**944**	**1,256**	**4,401**	**1,623**	**716**	**275**	**174**	**1,457**	**760**
Southwestern												
Clark	19	--	68	15	9	21	18	5	16	--	--	38
Fairfield	38	--	33	141	145	149	203	82	1	9	463	53
Fayette	1	31	12	23	--	1	--	3	--	--	--	3
Franklin	76	--	--	--	16	27	14	34	107	--	--	62
Greene	24	--	7	99	83	--	47	15	--	--	--	30
Licking	59	16	52	109	264	222	156	180	358	23	138	121
Madison	33	--	1	2	--	6	67	--	--	--	--	77
Pickaway	--	31	22	31	11	124	--	210	--	--	--	16
Total	**251**	**79**	**194**	**420**	**528**	**550**	**506**	**525**	**481**	**32**	**601**	**400**
Northwestern												
Champaign	--	--	25	81	32	17	9	25	--	--	--	48
Crawford	--	--	13	84	77	--	40	3	--	--	--	9
Delaware	9	1	1	41	21	2	--	--	--	--	--	28
Hancock	81	24	36	55	120	47	71	78	--	--	--	73
Hardin	38	1	1	4	1	78	78	--	--	--	--	--
Knox	27	174	113	26	56	196	69	47	47	11	171	44
Logan	25	45	--	--	167	--	74	--	--	--	81	--
Marion	76	0	11	11	--	127	86	--	--	7	--	--
Morrow	24	7	96	103	77	338	69	47	--	--	57	1
Sandusky	30	--	2	2	1	5	5	--	--	--	--	--
Seneca	16	--	20	27	65	59	7	10	--	--	--	21
Union	--	18	--	3	1	--	--	6	--	--	--	3
Williams	--	--	11	--	--	47	47	--	--	--	122	--
Wood	--	--	--	--	--	--	--	--	--	--	--	--
Wyandot	--	--	13	41	27	3	--	--	--	--	--	5
Total	**326**	**248**	**378**	**478**	**647**	**913**	**431**	**215**	**18**	**--**	**430**	**232**
State total	**1,496**	**1,352**	**8,089**	**19,289**	**18,200**	**31,849**	**22,195**	**35,508**	**7,014**	**2,609**	**55,174**	**10,854**

[a] Includes only those counties that supplied pulpwood in 2006.

All table cells without observations are indicated by --. Table value of 0 indicates the volume rounds to less than 1 standard cord, unpeeled.

Columns and rows may not add to their totals due to rounding.

Table 19.—Pulpwood production in standard cords, unpeeled, from roundwood by Forest Inventory Unit, county, and species group, Pennsylvania, 2006

Forest Inventory Unit and county[a]	All species	Species group												
		Hemlock	Shortleaf/loblolly pine	Red pine	White pine	Other pine	Spruce	Tama-rack	Ash	Aspen/balsam poplar	Bass-wood	Beech	White birch	Yellow birch
South Central														
Dauphin	6,168	83	--	--	13	25	--	--	333	--	37	6	--	--
Franklin	10,602	559	--	--	--	163	--	--	569	--	479	98	--	101
Fulton	11,565	273	--	--	2,907	3,743	--	--	166	50	140	16	--	--
Huntingdon	19,922	3,284	--	70	2,557	2,549	260	--	478	136	225	18	--	70
Juniata	11,783	1,984	301	--	747	2,074	--	--	181	22	414	135	--	--
Mifflin	3,779	422	--	--	1,193	38	--	--	26	--	4	25	--	2
Perry	4,407	533	--	--	768	646	--	--	106	--	36	38	--	--
Snyder	6,680	694	--	--	569	417	--	--	666	41	26	--	--	--
Union	7,689	88	--	0	17	--	--	--	575	--	311	136	76	176
Total	82,594	7,922	301	71	8,771	9,654	260	--	3,100	249	1,672	473	76	349
Western														
Allegheny	6,362	--	--	--	--	1,172	--	--	225	17	--	461	--	--
Armstrong	409	--	--	--	--	--	--	--	15	15	5	4	--	0
Beaver	36	--	--	--	--	--	--	--	0	0	--	2	--	--
Butler	1,869	--	--	--	--	--	--	--	23	162	5	--	--	--
Crawford	1,366	--	--	--	--	--	--	--	--	149	38	2	--	0
Erie	69	7	--	--	2	2	--	--	6	6	1	2	--	0
Greene	5,591	--	--	--	12	--	--	--	205	169	33	15	--	--
Indiana	7,478	466	--	24	103	100	--	--	105	341	286	185	--	34
Lawrence	199	--	--	--	163	--	--	--	0	2	2	2	--	0
Mercer	17,075	583	--	747	3,308	1,890	--	--	145	298	97	163	--	32
Washington	1,000	--	--	--	--	39	--	--	107	18	5	17	--	--
Westmoreland	8,773	31	--	15	21	--	--	--	100	332	109	6	--	0
Total	50,227	1,086	--	787	3,610	3,203	--	--	934	1,505	579	856	--	68
North Central/Allegheny														
Cameron	3,117	61	--	24	240	14	--	--	179	32	49	53	2	21
Centre	33,514	762	--	11	1,239	1,319	17	--	340	678	1,077	4	--	169
Clarion	4,765	99	--	--	120	98	--	--	58	274	13	275	--	9
Clearfield	60,302	7,563	--	1,197	7,880	531	--	--	810	1,621	953	951	2	125
Clinton	19,431	632	--	--	862	411	--	--	809	140	415	12	216	128
Elk	13,579	1,504	--	15	91	3	--	--	446	93	165	720	--	141
Forest	10,916	574	--	--	182	--	--	--	144	165	33	619	--	117
Jefferson	32,718	6,284	--	769	1,032	86	1,944	--	1,138	469	334	883	--	134
Lycoming	22,713	2,834	--	873	3,538	276	2	--	818	113	418	522	136	287
Mc Kean	70,130	992	--	--	13	--	2	--	3,095	1,105	1,659	5,064	--	1,007
Potter	38,231	18	--	15	365	724	--	--	1,808	562	553	2,948	2	345
Sullivan	10,864	4,210	--	--	3	1	--	9	498	52	158	385	--	164
Tioga	13,481	1,545	--	932	451	1	--	--	1,363	539	302	432	275	118
Venango	1,923	11	--	10	5	6	--	--	15	69	23	34	--	6
Warren	34,163	963	--	--	118	--	--	--	687	440	470	3,084	--	219
Total	369,845	28,052	--	3,846	16,139	3,468	1,964	9	12,208	6,354	6,621	15,986	634	2,989

Southwestern

County													
Bedford	31,517	1,101	57	--	1,896	4,532	--	--	804	124	214	11	--	--
Blair	4,829	21	--	34	333	9	--	13	243	4	89	49	--	9
Cambria	42,950	4,974	--	--	549	--	2,098	--	590	1,265	1,306	1,984	--	507
Fayette	12,165	--	--	--	39	19	--	--	88	32	613	24	--	5
Somerset	30,771	461	--	20	468	122	305	1	633	194	527	629	1	128
Total	**122,231**	**6,557**	**57**	**54**	**3,286**	**4,682**	**2,403**	**14**	**2,358**	**1,619**	**2,748**	**2,698**	**1**	**650**

Northeastern/Pocono

County													
Bradford	6,887	548	--	3	333	15	--	--	770	404	259	263	13	20
Carbon	549	51	--	0	14	3	--	--	--	9	--	30	--	--
Columbia	14,315	1,261	--	11	2,585	1,865	37	--	249	39	--	6	--	--
Lackawanna	3,582	14	--	--	--	0	8	--	254	218	13	188	--	16
Luzerne	9,225	1,076	--	--	821	126	--	--	252	217	191	58	51	85
Monroe	808	18	--	--	18	2	2	2	27	3	2	51	--	8
Montour	527	--	--	--	--	--	--	--	16	6	--	--	--	--
Northumberland	7,978	81	--	--	7	36	--	--	446	104	90	--	1	--
Pike	144	49	--	--	75	18	2	--	--	--	--	--	--	--
Schuylkill	13,803	332	--	--	105	50	8	--	581	567	258	83	3	3
Susquehanna	7,378	776	--	3	234	24	6	--	847	111	353	479	--	151
Wayne	7,704	819	--	20	8	10	3	--	766	139	199	472	--	243
Wyoming	3,458	645	--	--	349	--	2	--	223	94	31	177	150	44
Total	**76,357**	**5,670**	**--**	**38**	**4,548**	**2,151**	**67**	**2**	**4,431**	**1,910**	**1,397**	**1,809**	**218**	**570**

Southeastern

County													
Adams	6,510	94	--	--	1,058	172	--	--	228	--	--	82	--	--
Berks	4,342	38	--	--	--	91	134	--	547	37	--	2	--	4
Bucks	349	28	--	--	--	60	--	--	35	3	3	4	--	0
Chester	2,859	--	--	--	201	--	--	29	170	42	--	36	--	--
Cumberland	2,747	--	--	--	154	107	--	--	3	51	--	--	--	--
Delaware	3,033	145	--	--	284	299	95	39	1,959	--	--	--	--	--
Lancaster	3,736	83	--	--	163	173	55	22	313	--	--	97	--	--
Lebanon	6,695	122	--	--	--	160	55	154	468	121	--	17	--	66
Lehigh	420	--	--	2	6	--	--	9	55	18	--	--	--	--
Montgomery	234	24	--	--	46	49	16	6	26	--	1	--	--	--
Northampton	217	--	--	--	--	--	--	--	48	3	--	2	--	--
York	6,713	584	--	--	198	--	606	--	174	37	118	--	--	--
Total	**37,855**	**1,118**	**--**	**2**	**2,110**	**1,111**	**961**	**260**	**4,025**	**311**	**122**	**240**	**--**	**70**
State total	**739,110**	**50,405**	**358**	**4,797**	**38,463**	**24,269**	**5,655**	**285**	**27,056**	**11,949**	**13,138**	**22,061**	**929**	**4,698**

(Table 19 continued on next page)

(Table 19 continued)

Forest Inventory Unit and county[a]	Other birch	Black cherry	Black walnut	Cotton-wood	Elm	Hickory	Hard maple	Soft maple	Red oak group	White oak group	Sweet-gum	Syca-more	Tupelo/gum	Yellow-poplar	Other hard-woods
South Central															
Dauphin	561	166	51	--	5	131	154	494	1,473	1,370	--	--	109	1,081	77
Franklin	410	466	63	--	12	866	359	607	1,484	2,714	--	--	320	1,006	326
Fulton	266	130	1	--	78	275	204	349	1,218	1,249	--	--	166	159	176
Huntingdon	584	548	70	--	174	509	503	1,134	2,040	2,852	--	--	161	1,096	603
Juniata	594	159	35	--	335	246	459	583	1,088	824	--	294	146	762	399
Mifflin	183	--	--	--	--	37	--	229	687	893	--	--	42	23	--
Perry	118	35	43	--	4	159	41	265	630	727	--	--	58	128	85
Snyder	498	108	102	--	2	72	328	628	1,018	1,063	--	29	74	219	86
Union	1,168	256	10	--	24	74	33	1,036	1,677	1,441	--	--	87	502	86
Total	4,380	1,868	376	--	634	2,369	2,082	5,325	11,314	13,133	--	323	1,163	4,976	1,753
Western															
Allegheny	170	1,638	0	--	232	32	166	663	728	244	1	--	8	184	422
Armstrong	9	43	--	--	2	10	14	35	26	9	--	--	2	210	11
Beaver	1	12	0	--	2	--	3	3	3	1	--	0	11	0	3
Butler	10	278	--	--	8	11	3	542	302	63	--	--	11	422	27
Crawford	--	--	--	--	29	--	--	450	--	--	--	10	4	686	--
Erie	--	9	--	--	0	4	8	16	1	1	--	--	--	3	2
Greene	--	345	4	--	391	150	244	1,180	112	117	--	12	42	2,473	86
Indiana	180	924	--	--	113	107	456	893	489	192	--	13	22	2,227	218
Lawrence	0	5	1	--	1	2	2	8	6	0	--	2	2	0	1
Mercer	--	1,001	--	--	272	252	252	3,959	567	88	--	--	31	3,212	176
Washington	5	252	3	--	106	23	84	105	35	35	--	0	--	169	36
Westmoreland	240	425	1	--	323	24	123	2,409	243	179	--	23	140	3,898	91
Total	615	4,933	9	--	1,479	617	1,356	10,264	2,513	929	1	61	262	13,487	1,074
North Central/Allegheny															
Cameron	317	221	--	--	--	14	145	730	487	493	--	--	8	--	29
Centre	1,265	1,286	16	--	17	911	855	7,425	6,679	8,474	--	--	190	271	512
Clarion	387	696	2	--	0	50	37	1,301	813	419	--	--	11	23	79
Clearfield	2,697	5,398	--	2	6	346	4,498	12,806	5,823	4,271	--	--	232	1,045	1,545
Clinton	1,550	157	--	--	51	157	483	3,954	3,933	4,843	--	--	223	252	203
Elk	567	3,491	--	--	1	46	651	3,548	1,099	357	--	--	76	296	268
Forest	477	2,139	--	--	--	42	214	3,783	1,410	808	--	--	22	98	90
Jefferson	1,253	4,238	--	--	--	13	1,195	7,773	2,374	1,550	--	--	37	886	324
Lycoming	1,145	1,145	0	--	1	289	1,010	3,475	2,043	3,308	--	--	133	310	38
Mc Kean	1,521	21,820	--	--	44	262	8,964	20,309	3,051	328	--	--	4	603	288
Potter	1,060	6,777	--	--	14	--	9,952	11,406	2,451	140	--	--	--	64	112
Sullivan	330	1,322	--	--	--	53	348	1,751	226	136	--	--	--	135	8
Tioga	435	788	--	--	38	321	2,036	2,015	1,257	536	--	--	3	72	11
Venango	89	383	--	--	6	41	38	514	378	218	--	--	2	47	27
Warren	837	6,161	--	--	33	544	4,238	10,564	3,259	2,007	--	--	61	265	213
Total	13,931	56,021	18	2	212	3,088	34,665	91,353	35,284	27,887	--	--	1,001	4,366	3,748

Species group

Southwestern

County														
Bedford	645	1,734	4	136	322	960	2,492	2,622	4,874	4,601	18	266	1,681	2,423
Blair	372	590	1	--	131	125	251	773	860	547	--	56	181	138
Cambria	1,151	8,227	--	--	245	450	3,701	9,684	3,064	1,653	--	13	189	1,301
Fayette	299	941	--	--	184	26	106	3,372	459	640	136	214	4,775	194
Somerset	612	6,596	3	--	139	600	2,171	8,165	2,702	1,032	--	152	3,456	1,654
Total	3,078	18,087	7	136	1,021	2,161	8,721	24,615	11,959	8,472	154	700	10,282	5,711

Northeastern/Pocono

County														
Bradford	142	477	--	--	17	134	1,308	1,079	873	163	--	--	3	63
Carbon	16	13	--	1	--	0	0	167	70	155	--	9	--	10
Columbia	531	667	--	--	--	345	29	1,384	1,035	3,586	--	149	499	36
Lackawanna	85	143	--	--	5	75	356	1,041	497	466	--	19	151	33
Luzerne	733	244	--	9	6	131	314	1,632	1,267	1,623	--	90	159	140
Monroe	20	44	--	--	--	24	5	249	64	176	0	39	33	21
Montour	50	9	8	--	17	13	9	56	219	124	--	--	--	--
Northumberland	709	528	23	--	68	244	158	1,199	1,795	1,836	118	99	387	50
Pike	--	--	--	--	--	--	--	--	--	--	--	--	--	--
Schuylkill	1,213	68	27	--	--	149	5	1,851	2,009	4,884	--	389	900	317
Susquehanna	190	592	--	--	3	256	896	1,858	333	259	--	--	5	--
Wayne	519	632	--	--	12	28	1,179	2,231	139	230	--	--	55	--
Wyoming	119	96	--	--	2	13	370	898	174	41	--	1	16	11
Total	4,328	3,514	58	9	130	1,413	4,629	13,645	8,473	13,542	118	795	2,208	682

Southeastern

County														
Adams	134	398	47	--	3	511	3	461	1,162	1,595	--	137	240	185
Berks	99	194	103	--	12	194	5	467	525	443	4	63	1,246	132
Bucks	5	10	2	30	10	23	17	13	45	25	1	--	16	5
Chester	47	30	125	--	12	171	24	311	470	124	--	27	1,038	3
Cumberland	7	32	--	--	--	48	--	100	841	1,217	--	79	54	53
Delaware	--	48	78	--	--	85	--	--	--	--	--	--	--	--
Lancaster	312	101	24	--	16	145	--	289	373	770	--	29	656	114
Lebanon	422	323	18	--	15	83	18	898	1,216	1,431	--	125	660	322
Lehigh	23	11	34	--	--	16	19	7	119	14	7	1	65	15
Montgomery	--	--	13	--	0	13	1	2	21	1	--	--	7	8
Northampton	19	3	3	--	--	8	--	36	54	11	--	2	16	12
York	78	239	106	--	11	498	18	122	1,088	558	--	65	2,110	102
Total	1,146	1,390	554	30	81	1,796	104	2,706	5,915	6,191	13	528	6,107	951
State total	27,478	85,813	1,023	178	3,556	11,444	51,556	147,909	75,458	70,154	670	4,449	41,427	13,919

[a] Includes only those counties that supplied pulpwood in 2006.

All table cells without observations are indicated by --. Table value of 0 indicates the volume rounds to less than 1 standard cord, unpeeled.

Columns and rows may not add to their totals due to rounding.

Table 20.—Pulpwood production in standard cords, unpeeled, from roundwood by Forest Inventory Unit, county, and species group, West Virginia, 2006

Forest Inventory Unit and county[a]	All species	Hemlock	Shortleaf/ loblolly pine	Red pine	White pine	Other pine	Spruce	Ash	Aspen/ balsam poplar	Bass-wood	Beech	Yellow birch	Other birch
Northeastern													
Barbour	10,410	--	--	--	55	--	--	34	171	477	24	1	307
Berkeley	10,073	--	171	--	132	4,368	--	559	--	238	--	--	425
Braxton	19,771	6	--	--	321	--	--	333	--	884	860	36	262
Grant	20,931	9	64	--	2	57	--	343	207	4,161	243	46	103
Hampshire	22,894	414	64	--	1,050	3,279	--	268	12	188	62	--	134
Hardy	13,386	128	4	--	514	524	--	225	--	901	276	--	95
Harrison	13,021	--	--	--	--	--	--	173	195	16	--	--	--
Jefferson	1,066	--	--	--	--	--	--	231	--	44	--	--	110
Lewis	7,722	--	--	--	--	140	--	10	148	--	--	--	6
Mineral	9,856	122	129	--	1,019	1,313	--	446	1	486	267	14	11
Morgan	12,808	--	--	--	--	6,626	--	143	--	--	--	--	312
Pendleton	5,817	46	--	--	191	358	5	78	--	300	99	41	--
Pocahontas	36,617	161	98	--	2,064	131	161	450	348	6,141	1,667	340	1,980
Preston	30,192	9	9	15	79	--	--	140	91	910	1,080	148	1,078
Randolph	70,587	30	--	--	30	30	26	502	--	2,562	4,283	1,348	3,693
Taylor	1,896	--	--	--	--	--	--	14	--	33	2	--	6
Tucker	18,322	1,348	--	--	--	--	873	216	3	568	756	1,128	694
Upshur	27,188	--	--	--	22	21	--	13	--	181	208	57	1,539
Webster	38,914	--	--	--	--	121	--	76	271	5,216	1,637	199	1,948
Total	371,472	2,273	464	15	5,480	16,967	1,066	4,256	1,446	23,307	11,464	3,358	12,704
Southern													
Boone	9,177	--	--	--	--	141	--	--	--	990	345	--	454
Clay	7,279	169	--	--	--	477	--	3	--	643	290	--	185
Fayette	30,695	907	--	--	7	73	--	261	--	2,368	1,017	--	508
Greenbrier	86,785	49	68	18	1,323	572	6	2,381	0	1,586	1,959	1,021	1,567
Kanawha	9,257	--	--	--	--	1,141	--	13	--	1,301	578	--	30
Logan	4,668	--	5	--	111	26	--	--	--	756	421	--	18
McDowell	5,456	--	16	--	106	55	--	--	--	684	372	--	10
Mercer	5,309	2	--	47	509	183	--	46	--	749	156	--	13
Mingo	4,891	--	--	--	--	2	--	--	--	693	572	--	7
Monroe	13,157	--	--	--	1,277	693	--	243	--	267	654	--	404
Nicholas	76,788	247	--	--	199	89	--	586	--	5,685	1,163	680	2,403
Raleigh	15,276	2	--	--	485	--	--	209	20	1,177	427	29	173
Summers	3,790	2	--	--	536	295	--	142	--	246	116	--	7
Wyoming	5,958	--	--	--	33	--	--	--	--	355	649	--	13
Total	278,486	1,379	89	65	4,586	3,748	6	3,883	21	17,501	8,719	1,730	5,790

84

Northwestern

County													
Brooke	37	--	--	--	--	--	--	0	--	--	--	--	--
Cabell	2,473	--	--	--	--	1,092	--	10	--	2	66	--	--
Calhoun	3,543	--	27	--	39	383	--	3	21	304	44	--	--
Doddridge	11,066	--	--	--	12	27	--	63	883	147	423	--	5
Gilmer	4,467	--	--	--	--	110	--	1	--	225	180	--	36
Hancock	5	--	--	--	--	--	--	--	--	--	--	--	--
Jackson	8,108	--	40	--	--	2,156	--	49	27	48	93	--	--
Lincoln	3,151	--	--	--	--	231	--	--	--	101	488	--	10
Marion	8,196	--	--	--	--	--	--	134	703	228	28	--	--
Marshall	1,137	--	--	--	--	210	--	78	11	20	9	--	0
Mason	3,390	--	32	--	--	958	--	9	54	--	4	--	--
Monongalia	8,952	--	--	--	6	6	--	284	--	277	10	20	170
Ohio	699	--	--	--	--	--	--	1	--	--	1	--	--
Pleasants	1,443	--	--	--	170	286	--	17	182	66	52	--	--
Putnam	8,387	--	--	--	501	3,735	--	71	--	207	396	--	--
Ritchie	21,620	82	7	--	5,774	6,502	--	33	180	574	585	--	113
Roane	5,657	--	--	--	--	487	--	--	97	197	185	--	22
Tyler	2,033	--	--	--	--	13	--	44	65	97	37	--	10
Wayne	3,174	--	28	--	--	187	--	--	--	64	212	--	14
Wetzel	5,379	--	--	--	6	6	--	6	148	479	1	--	98
Wirt	17,836	--	2,692	--	4,311	8,400	--	4	--	--	64	--	--
Wood	14,387	--	--	--	--	6,515	--	123	722	182	184	--	--
Total	135,140	82	2,826	--	10,819	31,304	--	931	3,094	3,217	3,062	20	479
State total	785,099	3,734	3,379	80	20,885	52,019	1,071	9,070	4,561	44,025	23,244	5,109	18,973

(Table 20 continued on next page)

(Table 20 continued)

Forest Inventory Unit and county[a]	Black cherry	Black walnut	Elm	Hickory	Hard maple	Soft maple	Red oak group	White oak group	Sweet-gum	Syca-more	Tupelo/gum	Yellow-poplar	Other hard-woods
Northeastern													
Barbour	111	--	40	63	132	3,161	119	126	--	--	266	5,049	274
Berkeley	324	56	28	484	--	135	1,074	1,354	--	--	9	945	194
Braxton	35	3	116	990	725	1,470	1,914	2,023	--	1,012	122	7,490	1,004
Grant	653	--	391	432	1,493	2,848	1,401	1,713	--	10	390	5,887	384
Hampshire	163	--	198	1,425	62	1,099	3,504	8,877	--	198	488	1,155	287
Hardy	30	--	31	615	343	962	2,671	5,093	--	96	419	422	271
Harrison	182	1	457	245	190	2,111	65	66	--	2,190	199	6,321	240
Jefferson	110	--	2	60	--	16	101	20	--	226	--	129	128
Lewis	6	--	83	58	15	2,054	43	58	--	116	206	4,121	285
Mineral	374	--	68	757	1,012	537	1,444	2,507	--	--	61	348	246
Morgan	31	--	12	135	109	390	1,418	2,329	--	155	84	230	100
Pendleton	356	--	23	288	497	411	1,255	1,274	--	6	49	--	229
Pocahontas	911	--	123	261	717	8,346	959	633	--	--	29	10,493	600
Preston	2,260	--	149	990	1,736	6,625	3,442	1,337	--	90	325	8,723	964
Randolph	5,964	--	86	975	4,099	20,863	2,189	2,965	--	--	255	18,216	2,471
Taylor	19	--	--	36	29	621	61	52	--	--	33	978	14
Tucker	1,660	--	215	193	741	2,205	963	730	--	--	151	5,311	566
Upshur	96	0	28	271	228	6,908	358	409	--	1,315	265	15,009	261
Webster	433	--	128	250	526	7,620	646	725	--	89	339	17,874	815
Total	13,718	60	2,178	8,527	12,654	68,383	23,628	32,294	--	5,503	3,692	108,701	9,334
Southern													
Boone	--	--	162	--	--	1,035	--	--	--	888	257	4,557	348
Clay	0	--	33	18	11	1,466	25	37	--	--	132	3,534	256
Fayette	141	--	62	1,555	1,091	4,649	2,404	4,316	--	105	562	9,239	1,430
Greenbrier	3,183	--	270	4,754	4,027	10,307	12,307	18,126	--	67	292	16,276	6,627
Kanawha	4	--	58	61	39	1,184	76	105	--	116	183	3,724	645
Logan	--	--	4	--	--	357	--	--	--	10	68	2,595	297
McDowell	--	--	1	--	--	735	--	--	--	57	56	3,041	323
Mercer	63	--	4	157	57	599	331	310	--	--	80	1,675	330
Mingo	--	--	1	--	--	253	--	--	2	38	64	2,764	495
Monroe	124	--	199	523	342	746	2,174	2,670	--	--	42	1,774	1,028
Nicholas	378	--	29	698	1,777	9,229	1,379	3,340	72	262	658	46,675	1,238
Raleigh	154	--	1	250	501	2,524	960	1,003	--	--	134	5,983	1,243
Summers	9	--	42	123	77	455	332	336	--	--	107	550	414
Wyoming	--	--	1	--	--	729	--	--	--	19	49	3,528	581
Total	4,057	--	866	8,140	7,923	34,267	19,988	30,242	74	1,561	2,684	105,914	15,253

86

Northwestern

County												
Brooke	7	--	--	4	0	2	3	--	1	--	10	3
Cabell	--	31	17	29	195	24	138	--	110	48	624	86
Calhoun	0	41	16	6	436	12	22	--	112	31	1,920	123
Doddridge	49	33	347	209	2,425	366	477	--	27	188	4,960	424
Gilmer	1	140	21	4	721	16	21	--	234	37	2,601	115
Hancock	2	--	1	--	1	0	0	--	--	--	--	--
Jackson	59	164	299	213	930	913	987	--	72	183	1,610	265
Lincoln	--	2	--	--	582	--	--	--	153	53	1,423	107
Marion	166	135	209	180	1,683	398	334	--	329	34	3,431	202
Marshall	46	101	29	72	56	30	13	--	16	0	408	33
Mason	1	33	16	6	136	22	61	--	82	12	1,829	135
Monongalia	695	423	98	209	1,627	431	213	--	144	60	4,157	122
Ohio	2	278	--	5	4	1	--	--	55	--	349	2
Pleasants	0	28	37	22	70	51	31	--	136	2	195	97
Putnam	--	225	42	31	509	141	287	--	20	236	1,837	150
Ritchie	33	119	183	117	1,866	563	482	--	256	263	3,780	106
Roane	--	72	--	--	906	--	--	--	222	95	3,229	144
Tyler	23	58	77	55	354	70	79	--	11	33	984	22
Wayne	--	19	--	--	441	--	--	3	160	118	1,773	156
Wetzel	2	421	15	16	764	14	15	--	251	58	3,070	9
Wirt	3	54	22	5	362	64	109	--	137	8	1,468	131
Wood	176	176	365	306	1,106	860	1,602	--	271	256	931	609
Total	1,268	2,557	1,794	1,488	15,174	3,979	4,874	3	2,801	1,714	40,589	3,042
State total	19,044	5,601	18,462	22,065	117,824	47,594	67,410	78	9,865	8,090	255,204	27,629

[a] Includes only those counties that supplied pulpwood in 2006.

All table cells without observations are indicated by -- . Table value of 0 indicates the volume rounds to less than 1 standard cord, unpeeled.

Columns and rows may not add to their totals due to rounding.

Table 21.—Average production of active wood-pulp and composite product mills by company, location, and type of product produced, Mid-Atlantic States, 2006

Product and company	Location	Product produced	Average production
Pulp mills			
Luke Paper Co., Newpage Corp.	Luke, MD	Kraft pulp	1,200 tons pulp/day
Finch, Pruyn & Company, Inc.	Glens Falls, NY	Sulfite pulp	123 tons pulp/day
International Paper	Ticonderoga, NY	Kraft pulp	590 tons pulp/day
P. H. Glatfelter Co.	Chillicothe, OH	Kraft pulp	1,785 tons pulp/day
Smurfit-Stone	Coshocton, OH	Semichemical pulp	470 tons pulp/day
Appleton Papers, Inc.	Roaring Spring, PA	Kraft pulp	200 tons pulp/day
Glatfelter	Spring Grove, PA	Kraft pulp	700 tons pulp/day
Weyerhaeuser Co.	Johnsonburg, PA	Kraft pulp	231 tons pulp/day

Composite product mills

Great Lakes Mdf	Lacawanna, NY	Medium density fiberboard	120 million ft^2, 3/4-inch basis per year
Norbord Industries, Inc.	Deposit, NY	Medium density fiberboard	80 million ft^2, 3/4-inch basis per year
Inca Presswood Pallets, Ltd	Dover, OH	Molded compression board	na
Clarion Boards, Inc.	Shippenville, PA	Medium density fiber board	126 million ft^2, 3/4-inch basis per year
Craftmaster	Towanda, PA	Hardboard	na
Knight-Celotex, LLC	Sunbury, PA	Medium density fiber board	na
Temple-Inland	Kane, PA	Medium density fiber board	130 million ft^2, 3/4-inch basis per year
Werzalit Of America, Inc.	Bradford, PA	Particleboard	na
Georgia-Pacific Corp.	Mount Hope, WV	Oriented strand board	375 million ft^2, 3/4-inch basis per year
Jeld-Wen Wood Fiber	Craigsville, WV	Medium density fiberboard	na
Weyerhaeuser Co.	Heaters, WV	Oriented strand board	300 million ft^2, 3/4-inch basis per year
ILevel By Weyerhaeuser	Buckhannon, WV	Engineered wood products	na

Table 22.—Production and imports of pulpwood in standard cords, unpeeled, New England States, 2006

Product form, species group, and destination	Production by state[a]							Imports			Total receipts
	Connecticut	Maine	Massachusetts	New Hampshire	Rhode Island	Vermont	Regional Total	Mid-Atlantic States	Canada	Total imports	
Softwood roundwood											
Balsam fir											
Canada	--	33,042	--	--	--	--	33,042	--	--	--	--
Mid-Atlantic States	--	--	21	4,919	--	1,978	6,918	--	--	--	--
New England States	--	196,395	--	23,442	--	14,835	234,677	180	18,686	18,865	253,542
Total	--	229,437	24	28,361	--	16,814	274,636	180	18,686	18,865	253,542
Hemlock											
Canada	--	6,221	--	--	--	--	6,221	--	--	--	--
Mid-Atlantic States	501	--	3,920	32,629	--	9,658	46,708	--	--	--	--
New England States	--	207,675	3,808	24,663	--	24,040	260,187	365	4,400	4,765	264,952
Total	501	213,896	7,728	57,292	--	33,698	313,115	365	4,400	4,765	264,952
Jack pine											
Canada	--	18	--	--	--	--	18	--	--	--	--
Mid-Atlantic States	--	--	--	--	--	--	--	--	--	--	--
New England States	--	7	--	--	--	--	7	--	1	1	8
Total	--	25	--	--	--	--	25	--	1	1	8
Red pine											
Canada	--	932	--	--	--	--	932	--	--	--	--
Mid-Atlantic States	--	--	--	--	--	--	--	--	--	--	--
New England States	--	11,813	17	629	--	356	12,815	33	2,305	2,338	15,153
Total	--	12,745	17	629	--	356	13,746	33	2,305	2,338	15,153
White pine											
Canada	--	6,890	--	--	--	--	6,890	--	--	--	--
Mid-Atlantic States	589	--	1,606	138	34	11,737	14,103	--	--	--	--
New England States	4	143,886	10,760	30,985	293	14,205	200,134	569	3,550	4,119	204,254
Total	593	150,776	12,366	31,122	327	25,943	221,127	569	3,550	4,119	204,254
Other pine											
New England States	--	1,039	5,230	511	34	95	6,908	13	30	44	6,952
Total	--	1,039	5,230	511	34	95	6,908	13	30	44	6,952
Spruce											
Canada	--	75,031	--	--	--	--	75,031	--	--	--	--
Mid-Atlantic States	16	--	385	10,769	--	4,485	15,655	--	--	--	--
New England States	--	332,848	60	24,449	--	16,875	374,233	276	34,766	35,042	409,274
Total	16	407,879	445	35,218	--	21,360	464,919	276	34,766	35,042	409,274
Tamarack											
Canada	--	796	--	--	--	--	796	--	--	--	--
New England States	--	13,793	--	1,773	--	656	16,222	--	4,125	4,125	20,347
Total	--	14,589	--	1,773	--	656	17,018	--	4,125	4,125	20,347

Total softwood roundwood

Canada	—	122,929	—	—	—	—	122,929	—	—	—	—
Mid-Atlantic States	1,105	—	5,931	48,454	34	27,858	83,383	—	—	—	—
New England States	4	907,457	19,879	106,453	327	71,063	1,105,183	1,435	67,863	69,299	1,174,482
Total	1,110	1,030,386	25,810	154,907	361	98,921	1,311,495	1,435	67,863	69,299	1,174,482

Softwood residues

Canada	—	64,666	—	—	—	—	64,666	—	—	—	—
Mid-Atlantic States	—	—	1,381	1,284	—	7,670	10,336	—	—	—	—
New England States	—	299,998	781	53,978	—	2,959	357,714	—	74,878	74,878	432,593
Total	—	364,664	2,162	55,262	—	10,629	432,716	—	74,878	74,878	432,593

Total softwood material

Canada	—	187,595	—	—	—	—	187,595	—	—	—	—
Mid-Atlantic States	1,105	—	7,313	49,738	34	35,528	93,719	—	—	—	—
New England States	4	1,207,455	20,660	160,431	327	74,021	1,462,898	1,435	142,742	144,177	1,607,074
Total	1,110	1,395,050	27,972	210,169	361	109,550	1,744,211	1,435	142,742	144,177	1,607,074

(Table 22 continued on next page)

(Table 22 continued)

Product form, species group, and destination	Production by state[a]							Imports			Total receipts
	Connecticut	Maine	Massa- chusetts	New Hampshire	Rhode Island	Vermont	Regional Total	Mid-Atlantic States	Canada	Total imports	
Hardwood roundwood											
Ash											
Canada	—	4,685	—	1,274	—	364	6,323	—	—	—	—
Mid-Atlantic States	58	—	172	134	0	1,251	1,615	—	—	—	—
New England States	3	69,844	0	4,241	2	1,971	76,062	—	7,727	7,727	83,789
Total	61	74,528	172	5,650	3	3,585	84,000	—	7,727	7,727	83,789
Aspen/balsam poplar											
Canada	—	2,176	—	—	—	225	2,400	—	—	—	—
Mid-Atlantic States	16	—	61	93	—	457	627	—	—	—	—
New England States	—	387,695	158	9,637	—	5,546	403,035	61	200,301	200,362	603,398
Total	16	389,871	218	9,730	—	6,227	406,063	61	200,301	200,362	603,398
Basswood											
Canada	—	334	—	46	—	23	402	—	—	—	—
Mid-Atlantic States	—	—	—	—	—	—	—	—	—	—	—
New England States	—	4,261	—	188	—	158	4,608	—	222	222	4,830
Total	—	4,595	—	234	—	181	5,010	—	222	222	4,830
Beech											
Canada	—	7,349	—	2,431	—	274	10,053	—	—	—	—
Mid-Atlantic States	149	—	479	248	2	1,801	2,679	—	—	—	—
New England States	4	157,836	—	8,272	—	1,977	168,089	—	50,684	50,684	218,772
Total	153	165,185	479	10,950	2	4,052	180,821	—	50,684	50,684	218,772
White birch											
Canada	—	12,450	—	3,058	—	335	15,843	—	—	—	—
Mid-Atlantic States	60	—	204	254	1	1,385	1,904	—	—	—	—
New England States	—	187,080	130	22,686	—	4,174	214,070	—	62,634	62,634	276,703
Total	60	199,530	334	25,998	1	5,894	231,817	—	62,634	62,634	276,703
Yellow birch											
Canada	—	13,299	—	2,884	—	463	16,646	—	—	—	—
Mid-Atlantic States	92	—	289	230	1	1,888	2,499	—	—	—	—
New England States	0	179,215	204	25,077	1	4,835	209,333	—	30,911	30,911	240,244
Total	92	192,515	493	28,191	2	7,185	228,478	—	30,911	30,911	240,244
Other birch											
Canada	—	198	—	71	—	23	292	—	—	—	—
Mid-Atlantic States	—	—	—	—	—	—	—	—	—	—	—
New England States	6	6,410	363	2,980	1	918	10,678	—	1,382	1,382	12,061
Total	6	6,609	363	3,051	1	940	10,970	—	1,382	1,382	12,061
Black cherry											
Canada	38	167	110	81	0	124	372	—	—	—	—
Mid-Atlantic States	—	—	—	50	—	527	726	—	—	—	—
New England States	2	3,910	187	743	0	799	5,641	—	318	318	5,958
Total	40	4,077	297	875	0	1,449	6,738	—	318	318	5,958

Elm

Canada	--	66	--	6	--	20	92	--	--	--	--
New England States	--	1,444	--	36	1	110	1,591	--	98	98	1,689
Total	--	1,510	--	42	1	130	1,683	--	98	98	1,689

Hickory

New England States	3	--	--	40	--	18	61	--	31	31	93
Total	3	--	--	40	--	18	61	--	31	31	93

Hard maple

Canada	--	19,595	--	4,321	--	1,532	25,448	--	--	--	--
Mid-Atlantic States	122	--	376	330	1	4,280	5,109	--	--	--	--
New England States	3	284,865	225	35,438	--	18,380	338,911	--	62,039	62,039	400,950
Total	125	304,460	600	40,089	1	24,192	369,468	--	62,039	62,039	400,950

Soft maple

Canada	--	23,805	--	5,336	--	1,039	30,180	--	--	--	--
Mid-Atlantic States	176	--	456	440	2	3,518	4,592	--	--	--	--
New England States	8	459,773	1,596	48,496	35	12,022	521,930	--	133,604	133,604	655,535
Total	184	483,578	2,053	54,272	36	16,579	556,703	--	133,604	133,604	655,535

Red oak group

Canada	1	3,085	--	1,947	--	56	5,088	--	--	--	--
Mid-Atlantic States	91	--	122	127	0	844	1,185	--	--	--	--
New England States	13	59,043	4,024	7,272	32	955	71,339	--	6,824	6,824	78,163
Total	105	62,128	4,146	9,346	32	1,855	77,612	--	6,824	6,824	78,163

White oak group

Canada	--	27	--	73	--	--	101	--	--	--	--
Mid-Atlantic States	25	--	78	40	0	294	438	--	--	--	--
New England States	2	1,359	1104	445	10	36	2,957	--	229	229	3,186
Total	27	1,387	1,182	559	10	330	3,495	--	229	229	3,186

Other hardwoods

Canada	1	3	--	3	--	--	6	--	--	--	--
New England States	--	84	137	4	--	73	298	--	12	12	310
Total	1	87	137	7	--	73	304	--	12	12	310

(Table 22 continued on next page)

(Table 22 continued)

| Product form, species group, and destination | Production by state[a] | | | | | | | Imports | | | Total receipts |
	Connecticut	Maine	Massa-chusetts	New Hampshire	Rhode Island	Vermont	Regional Total	Mid-Atlantic States	Canada	Total imports	
Total hardwood roundwood											
Canada	--	87,239	--	21,530	--	4,476	113,246	--	--	--	--
Mid-Atlantic States	827	--	2,346	1,946	9	16,244	21,373	--	--	--	--
New England States	47	1,802,820	8,129	165,556	81	51,972	2,028,604	61	557,016	557,077	2,585,681
Total	875	1,890,058	10,475	189,033	90	72,692	2,163,223	61	557,016	557,077	2,585,681
Hardwood residues											
Canada	--	7,214	--	5,160	--	3,607	15,982	--	--	--	--
Mid-Atlantic States	1,422	--	239	1,310	--	14,635	17,606	--	--	--	--
New England States	--	155,141	--	1,623	--	--	156,765	--	31,996	31,996	188,760
Total	1,422	162,355	239	8,094	--	18,242	190,353	--	31,996	31,996	188,760
Total hardwood material											
Canada	--	94,453	--	26,691	--	8,084	129,227	--	--	--	--
Mid-Atlantic States	2,250	--	2,585	3,257	9	30,879	38,979	--	--	--	--
New England States	47	1,957,961	8,129	167,180	81	51,972	2,185,369	61	589,012	589,073	2,774,442
Total	2,297	2,052,414	10,714	197,127	90	90,934	2,353,576	61	589,012	589,073	2,774,442
Total all roundwood											
Canada	--	210,168	--	21,530	--	4,476	236,175	--	--	--	--
Mid-Atlantic States	1,933	--	8,277	50,400	43	44,102	104,756	--	--	--	--
New England States	51	2,710,277	28,008	272,009	408	123,034	3,133,788	1,496	624,880	626,376	3,760,163
Total	1,984	2,920,444	36,286	343,940	451	171,613	3,474,718	1,496	624,880	626,376	3,760,163
Total all residues											
Canada	--	71,880	--	5,160	--	3,607	80,648	--	--	--	--
Mid-Atlantic States	1,422	--	1,621	2,595	--	22,305	27,942	--	--	--	--
New England States	--	455,139	781	55,601	--	2,959	514,479	--	106,874	106,874	621,353
Total	1,422	527,019	2,401	63,356	--	28,871	623,069	--	106,874	106,874	621,353
Total all wood material											
Canada	--	282,048	--	26,691	--	8,084	316,822	--	--	--	--
Mid-Atlantic States	3,355	--	9,898	52,995	43	66,407	132,698	--	--	--	--
New England States	51	3,165,416	28,789	327,610	408	125,993	3,648,267	1,496	731,754	733,250	4,381,516
Total	3,406	3,447,464	38,687	407,296	451	200,484	4,097,787	1,496	731,754	733,250	4,381,516

[a] Vertical columns of figures under the box heading "Production by State" present the amount of roundwood cut or residue generated in each state

All table cells without observations are indicated by -- . Table value of 0 indicates the volume rounds to less than 1 standard cord, unpeeled. Columns and rows may not add to their totals due to rounding.

Table 23.—New England States pulpwood production in thousand standard cords, unpeeled, from roundwood by state and species group, 2001-2006 [a]

State	All species 2001	All species 2005	All species 2006	Pine 2001	Pine 2005	Pine 2006
Connecticut	4	4	2	—	2	1
Maine	3,310	2,680	2,920	—	106	165
Massachusetts	19	37	36	—	15	18
New Hampshire	286	478	344	—	67	32
Rhode Island	1	0	0	—	0	0
Vermont	185	214	172	—	38	26
Total New England States	3,804	3,414	3,475	—	229	242

State	Spruce/balsam fir 2001 [b]	Spruce/balsam fir 2005	Spruce/balsam fir 2006	Hemlock/tamarack 2001	Hemlock/tamarack 2005	Hemlock/tamarack 2006	Aspen/balsam poplar 2001	Aspen/balsam poplar 2005	Aspen/balsam poplar 2006	Beech 2001	Beech 2005	Beech 2006
Connecticut	3	0	0	—	1	1	—	0	0	—	0	0
Maine	1,209	562	637	—	186	228	—	386	390	—	145	165
Massachusetts	17	0	0	—	5	8	—	2	0	—	0	0
New Hampshire	133	55	64	—	25	59	—	54	10	—	11	11
Rhode Island	1	—	—	—	—	—	—	—	—	—	0	0
Vermont	99	27	38	—	24	34	—	26	6	—	3	4
Total New England States	1,462	643	740	—	241	330	—	469	406	—	159	181

State	Birch 2001	Birch 2005	Birch 2006	Maple 2001	Maple 2005	Maple 2006	Other hardwoods 2001 [c]	Other hardwoods 2005	Other hardwoods 2006
Connecticut	—	0	0	—	0	0	1	0	0
Maine	—	391	399	—	773	788	2,101	131	148
Massachusetts	—	2	1	—	7	3	2	5	6
New Hampshire	—	78	57	—	177	94	153	13	17
Rhode Island	—	0	0	—	0	0	0	0	0
Vermont	—	23	14	—	67	41	86	6	8
Total New England States	—	494	471	—	1,024	926	2,342	155	179

[a] Data is not available for 2002, 2003, and 2004.

[b] Includes all softwoods in 2001.

[c] Includes all hardwoods in 2001.

All table cells without observations are indicated by — . Table value of 0 indicates the volume rounds to less than 1 standard cord, unpeeled. Columns and rows may not add to their totals due to rounding.

Table 24.—Pulpwood production in standard cords, unpeeled, by mill type, product form, state of origin, and species group. New England States, 2006

| Product form and species group | All States | State of origin for pulp products | | | | | | State of origin for composite products |
		Connecticut	Maine	Massachusetts	New Hampshire	Rhode Island	Vermont	Maine
Softwood roundwood								
Balsam fir	274,628	—	229,429	24	28,361	—	16,814	8
Hemlock	313,115	501	213,896	7,728	57,292	—	33,698	—
Jack pine	25	—	25	—	—	—	—	—
Red pine	8,074	—	7,073	17	629	—	356	5,672
White pine	221,027	593	150,676	12,366	31,122	327	25,943	100
Other pine	6,908	—	1,039	5,230	511	34	95	—
Spruce	464,910	16	407,870	445	35,218	—	21,360	9
Tamarack	13,482	—	11,053	—	1,773	—	656	3,536
Total softwood roundwood	1,302,170	1,110	1,021,061	25,810	154,907	361	98,921	9,325
Hardwood roundwood								
Ash	84,000	61	74,528	172	5,650	3	3,585	—
Aspen/balsam poplar	267,816	16	251,624	218	9,730	—	6,227	138,247
Basswood	5,010	—	4,595	—	234	2	181	—
Beech	180,821	153	165,185	479	10,950	2	4,052	—
White birch	231,817	60	199,530	334	25,998	1	5,894	—
Yellow birch	228,478	92	192,515	493	28,191	2	7,185	—
Other birch	10,970	6	6,609	363	3,051	1	940	—
Black cherry	6,738	40	4,077	297	875	0	1,449	—
Elm	1,683	—	1,510	—	42	1	130	—
Hickory	61	3	—	—	40	1	18	—
Hard maple	369,468	125	304,460	600	40,089	1	24,192	—
Soft maple	538,265	184	465,140	2,053	54,272	36	16,579	18,438
Red oak group	77,612	105	62,128	4,146	9,346	32	1,855	—
White oak group	3,495	27	1,387	1,182	559	10	330	—
Other hardwoods	304	1	87	137	7	—	73	—
Total hardwood roundwood	2,006,538	875	1,733,373	10,475	189,033	90	72,692	156,685
Total Roundwood	3,308,708	1,984	2,754,434	36,286	343,940	451	171,613	166,010
Residues								
Softwood	432,716	—	364,664	2,162	55,262	—	10,629	—
Hardwood	190,353	1,422	162,355	239	8,094	—	18,242	—
Total residues	623,069	1,422	527,019	2,401	63,356	—	28,871	—
State total	3,931,777	3,406	3,281,454	38,687	407,296	451	200,484	166,010

All table cells without observations are indicated by — . Table value of 0 indicates the volume rounds to less than 1 standard cord, unpeeled. Columns and rows may not add to their totals due to rounding.

Table 25.—Pulpwood production in standard cords, unpeeled, by mill type, product form, species group, and percent change, New England States, 2005 and 2006

Product form and species group	Pulp mills			Composite mills		
	2005	2006	Percent change	2005	2006	Percent change
Softwood roundwood						
Balsam fir	221,265	274,628	24%	--	8	--
Hemlock	226,297	313,115	38%	2,434	--	--
Jack pine	23	25	9%	15	--	--
Red pine	6,836	8,074	18%	1,340	5,672	323%
White pine	210,574	221,027	5%	3,524	100	-97%
Other pine	6,596	6,908	5%	--	--	--
Spruce	422,071	464,910	10%	--	9	--
Tamarack	11,288	13,482	19%	1,388	3,536	155%
Total softwood roundwood	1,104,948	1,302,170	18%	8,701	9,325	7%
Hardwood roundwood						
Ash	74,335	84,000	13%	698	--	--
Aspen/balsam poplar	304,767	267,816	-12%	163,865	138,247	-16%
Basswood	3,673	5,010	36%	--	--	--
Beech	157,826	180,821	15%	1,544	--	--
White birch	235,395	231,817	-2%	2,734	--	--
Yellow birch	236,380	228,478	-3%	3,930	--	--
Other birch	15,428	10,970	-29%	33	--	--
Black cherry	5,830	6,738	16%	26	--	--
Elm	1,303	1,683	29%	8	--	--
Hickory	55	61	11%	--	--	--
Hard maple	416,173	369,468	-11%	8,064	--	--
Soft maple	594,643	538,265	-9%	5,004	18,438	268%
Red oak group	65,876	77,612	18%	36	--	--
White oak group	2,946	3,495	19%	--	--	--
Other hardwoods	273	304	11%	--	--	--
Total hardwood roundwood	2,114,901	2,006,538	-5%	185,942	156,685	-16%
Total Roundwood	3,219,849	3,308,708	3%	194,643	166,010	-15%
Residues						
Softwood	621,504	432,716	-30%	--	--	--
Hardwood	183,170	190,353	4%	--	--	--
Total residues	804,674	623,069	-23%	--	--	--
State total	4,024,523	3,931,777	-2%	194,643	166,010	-15%

All table cells without observations are indicated by --. Table value of 0 indicates the volume rounds to less than 1 standard cord, unpeeled. Columns and rows may not add to their totals due to rounding.

Table 26.—Pulpwood production in standard cords, unpeeled, from roundwood by state, county, and species group, Connecticut, Massachusetts, and Rhode Island, 2006

State and county[a]	All species	Species group								
		Balsam fir	Hemlock	Red pine	White pine	Other pine	Spruce	Ash	Aspen/ balsam poplar	Beech
CONNECTICUT										
Fairfield	670	--	--	--	145	--	--	35	10	115
Hartford	11	--	11	--	--	--	--	--	--	--
Litchfield	615	--	298	--	32	--	10	22	4	21
New London	11	--	--	--	11	--	--	--	--	--
Tolland	305	--	176	--	130	--	--	--	--	--
Windham	372	--	17	--	275	--	6	5	2	17
Connecticut total	1,984	--	501	--	593	--	16	61	16	153
MASSACHUSETTS										
Barnstable	12,719	--	1,646	--	228	5,211	--	1	18	3
Berkshire	2,862	20	823	--	478	--	185	107	35	278
Essex	885	--	254	--	632	--	--	--	--	--
Franklin	4,094	4	1,582	6	1,248	8	86	20	51	67
Hampden	2,229	--	1,443	--	374	--	50	23	12	66
Hampshire	1,941	--	932	--	633	--	70	21	6	65
Middlesex	3,528	--	162	--	3,051	5	--	0	33	--
Plymouth	64	--	--	--	27	3	--	--	--	--
Worcester	7,963	0	886	11	5,696	4	54	0	64	--
Massachusetts total	36,286	24	7,728	17	12,366	5,230	445	172	218	479
RHODE ISLAND										
Bristol	408	--	--	--	293	34	--	2	--	--
Kent	21	--	--	--	21	--	--	--	--	--
Providence	21	--	--	--	12	--	--	0	--	2
Rhode Island total	451	--	--	--	327	34	--	3	--	2

State and County[a]	White fir	Yellow fir	Other fir	Balsam err	Elm	Minor	Hard maple	Soft maple	Red oak group	White oak group	Other hardwoods
CONNECTICUT											
Fairfield	44	64	6	19	--	3	83	93	30	21	1
Hartford	--	--	--	--	--	--	--	--	--	--	--
Litchfield	9	18	--	18	--	--	30	78	72	3	--
New London	--	--	--	--	--	--	--	--	--	--	--
Tolland	--	--	--	--	--	--	--	--	--	--	--
Windham	7	10	--	3	--	--	12	13	3	3	--
Connecticut total	60	92	6	40	--	3	125	184	105	27	1
MASSACHUSETTS											
Barnstable	1	2	--	187	--	--	3	176	4,008	1,100	136
Berkshire	119	168	--	67	--	--	218	259	60	45	--
Essex	--	--	--	--	--	--	--	--	--	--	--
Franklin	81	157	241	12	--	--	160	348	14	11	--
Hampden	29	40	--	17	--	--	56	78	31	11	--
Hampshire	27	39	--	13	--	--	50	59	14	11	--
Middlesex	5	21	39	--	--	--	3	205	4	1	--
Plymouth	--	0	0	1	--	--	--	16	13	4	1
Worcester	72	66	82	0	--	--	111	913	3	--	--
Massachusetts total	334	493	363	297	--	--	600	2,053	4,146	1,182	137
RHODE ISLAND											
Bristol	--	1	1	--	1	--	--	35	32	10	--
Kent	--	--	--	--	--	--	--	--	--	--	--
Providence	1	1	--	0	--	--	1	2	0	0	--
Rhode Island total	1	2	1	0	1	--	1	36	32	10	--

[a] Includes only those counties that supplied pulpwood in 2006.

All table cells without observations are indicated by --. Table value of 0 indicates the volume rounds to less than 1 standard cord, unpeeled.

Columns and rows may not add to their totals due to rounding.

Table 27.—Pulpwood production in standard cords, unpeeled, from roundwood by county and species group, Maine, 2006

County[a]	All species	Balsam fir	Hemlock	Jack pine	Red pine	White pine	Other pine	Spruce	Tamarack	Ash	Aspen balsam poplar	Basswood
Androscoggin	61,459	465	6,025	--	29	14,276	--	93	--	3,675	3,307	633
Aroostook	412,559	20,871	8,332		2,839	250	--	37,106	5,282	3,852	141,017	--
Cumberland	53,120	607	10,984		191	17,161	666	310	--	1,782	1,333	85
Franklin	261,966	28,050	10,819		--	7,762	--	17,805	347	8,258	28,345	1,001
Hancock	129,357	7,090	18,373		1,153	4,652	--	31,692	295	2,351	12,482	74
Kennebec	52,739	4,432	8,021		91	14,311	--	457	47	2,261	8,212	170
Knox	15,336	1,768	743		17	1,816	--	5,536	7	192	1,495	--
Lincoln	18,727	2,948	1,632		--	6,224	--	2,275	14	113	1,814	--
Oxford	313,050	19,890	34,532		828	29,936	135	25,608	134	10,405	14,468	40
Penobscot	378,825	31,061	39,028	20	1,155	10,873		72,354	1,777	10,669	47,554	127
Piscataquis	308,242	31,220	15,785		278	3,223		83,677	1,710	6,248	35,759	666
Sagadahoc	6,550	159	990		3,003	2,270	139	566	2	118	673	--
Somerset	547,341	50,243	25,651			17,452	--	73,086	3,561	18,692	60,733	1,647
Waldo	70,278	11,681	8,822		--	5,170	--	9,651	849	2,086	8,073	139
Washington	243,112	18,848	12,907	5	2,803	2,598	--	47,616	499	2,533	23,491	--
York	47,784	105	11,252		358	12,803	99	48	64	1,294	1,116	11
Maine total	2,920,444	229,437	213,896	25	12,745	150,776	1,039	407,879	14,589	74,528	389,871	4,595

County[a]	Beech	White birch	Yellow birch	Other birch	Black cherry	Elm	Hard maple	Soft maple	Red oak group	White oak group	Other hardwoods
Androscoggin	2,006	3,567	359	54	257	202	1,686	16,472	8,332	22	--
Aroostook	29,896	18,613	27,036	162	54	45	64,062	52,599	545	--	--
Cumberland	1,802	1,327	382	183	66	110	450	8,899	6,446	336	--
Franklin	7,936	36,778	31,474	210	165	--	35,554	44,203	3,258	--	--
Hancock	7,459	8,427	3,375	241	--	26	5,696	23,500	2,473	--	--
Kennebec	1,635	1,693	739	126	61	36	1,065	5,300	4,077	7	--
Knox	160	666	248	--	16	8	112	1,612	942	--	--
Lincoln	116	471	94	35	32	2	66	1,937	911	43	--
Oxford	20,507	20,716	29,081	209	322	179	34,527	53,471	17,876	185	--
Penobscot	26,758	22,093	19,227	1,479	938	245	24,442	64,220	4,449	293	65
Piscataquis	15,239	17,912	23,194	162	199	101	36,820	34,767	1,281	--	--
Sagadahoc	26	95	79	2	14	4	60	881	462	11	--
Somerset	23,704	44,423	46,293	1,340	825	356	90,828	84,582	900	--	22
Waldo	1,583	3,453	880	20	1,052	170	2,351	11,550	2,685	63	--
Washington	25,516	18,390	9,630	1,757	58	--	6,316	69,197	948	--	--
York	844	906	426	629	20	27	425	10,388	6,542	427	--
Maine total	165,185	199,530	192,515	6,609	4,077	1,510	304,460	483,578	62,128	1,387	87

[a] Includes only those counties that supplied pulpwood in 2006.
All table cells without observations are indicated by --. Table value of 0 indicates the volume rounds to less than 1 standard cord, unpeeled.
Columns and rows may not add to their totals due to rounding.

Table 28.—Pulpwood production in standard cords, unpeeled, from roundwood by state, Forest Inventory Unit, county, and species group, New Hampshire and Vermont, 2006

State, Forest Inventory Unit, and county[a]	All species	Balsam fir	Hemlock	Red pine	White pine	Species group Other pine	Spruce	Tamarack	Ash	Aspen/ balsam poplar	Basswood
NEW HAMPSHIRE											
Northern											
Carroll	50,713	1,826	12,726	197	3,886	458	6,037	16	1,340	386	21
Coos	125,558	14,236	3,757	--	1,628	--	12,012	1,705	1,584	5,790	--
Grafton	69,786	11,348	9,780	176	3,341	16	10,871	--	1,726	1,893	92
Total	246,058	27,410	26,263	374	8,855	474	28,921	1,721	4,651	8,069	113
Southern											
Be knap	7,280	38	1,944	41	2,177	--	176	--	52	93	32
Cheshire	10,828	95	1,908	7	1,827	--	520	--	132	347	4
Hillsborough	14,523	11	2,022	152	5,893	37	102	5	154	29	16
Merrimack	44,288	625	22,430	17	5,479	--	4,684	--	390	516	35
Rockingham	8,288	--	720	21	3,684	--	11	48	64	320	19
Strafford	4,595	3	998	18	1,553	--	110	--	61	101	6
Sullivan	8,081	179	1,008	--	1,655	--	695	--	145	255	7
Total	97,883	951	31,029	255	22,268	37	6,298	52	999	1,661	121
New Hampshire total	343,940	28,361	57,292	629	31,122	511	35,218	1,773	5,650	9,730	234
VERMONT											
Northern											
Caledonia	29,421	2,500	4,981	--	1,881	76	2,292	533	712	2,137	--
Essex	11,967	3,994	674	--	365	--	2,837	8	108	431	10
Franklin	10,354	563	3,324	--	1,470	--	526	56	198	121	2
Grand Isle	127	--	39	--	41	--	--	--	28	--	4
Lamoille	8,298	1,415	2,008	--	772	--	1,068	--	100	49	--
Orange	17,465	1,551	5,150	--	1,972	--	2,119	--	306	879	86
Orleans	11,878	3,919	964	--	912	--	2,752	13	139	607	8
Washington	10,840	833	1,787	--	1,402	19	2,462	44	225	542	14
Total	100,350	14,775	18,927	--	8,816	95	14,056	653	1,817	4,766	125
Southern											
Addison	5,939	300	613	--	1,294	--	834	--	93	129	11
Bennington	8,251	433	413	--	1,490	--	972	--	340	57	--
Chittenden	4,238	14	395	--	1,062	--	28	--	168	231	14
Rutland	15,391	683	3,123	--	5,006	--	1,601	--	451	200	9
Windham	19,302	566	4,537	356	4,801	--	2,286	3	237	71	5
Windsor	18,142	43	5,691	--	3,473	--	1,583	--	480	774	18
Total	71,263	2,039	14,771	356	17,127	--	7,304	3	1,768	1,462	56
Vermont total	171,613	16,814	33,698	356	25,943	95	21,360	656	3,585	6,227	181

(Table 28 continued on next page)

(Table 28 continued)

						Species group						
State, Forest Inventory Unit, and county[a]	Beech	White birch	Yellow birch	Other birch	Black cherry	Elm	Hickory	Hard maple	Soft maple	Red oak group	White oak group	Other hardwoods
NEW HAMPSHIRE												
Northern												
Carroll	3,218	1,818	2,564	209	52	--	--	4,421	7,611	3,693	233	--
Coos	4,342	14,294	19,957	213	501	12	--	26,390	18,573	566	--	--
Grafton	2,525	6,762	3,752	35	96	12	--	6,118	9,511	1,709	16	7
Total	10,084	22,874	26,273	457	649	24	--	36,929	35,694	5,968	249	7
Southern												
Belknap	70	354	200	52	17	1	--	391	1,339	300	1	--
Cheshire	176	594	248	617	61	1	14	455	3,120	697	5	--
Hillsborough	78	387	194	551	40	2	3	230	3,894	636	87	--
Merrimack	296	1,058	538	662	61	2	--	664	5,501	1,187	142	--
Rockingham	60	148	108	410	19	12	16	175	2,110	305	38	--
Strafford	126	11	177	157	4	--	6	231	845	153	36	--
Sullivan	59	573	453	144	25	1	--	1,013	1,769	100	--	--
Total	866	3,124	1,918	2,594	226	19	40	3,160	18,578	3,379	309	--
New Hampshire total	10,950	25,998	28,191	3,051	875	42	40	40,089	54,272	9,346	559	7
VERMONT												
Northern												
Caledonia	780	946	1,747	12	447	44	--	5,616	4,580	44	22	72
Essex	111	472	683	2	19	1	--	1,442	808	1	--	--
Franklin	265	261	418	28	83	21	--	1,464	1,431	85	36	--
Grand Isle	--	--	--	--	--	2	--	--	12	--	0	--
Lamoille	211	146	399	11	79	4	--	1,111	892	15	17	--
Orange	299	433	398	2	80	37	--	3,155	619	367	10	--
Orleans	95	314	349	20	61	1	--	1,267	443	7	8	--
Washington	226	525	401	7	71	2	--	1,284	929	55	14	--
Total	1,987	3,098	4,396	83	840	112	--	15,339	9,714	574	107	72
Southern												
Addison	179	292	350	94	35	4	2	1,025	593	67	25	--
Bennington	306	219	632	35	140	--	--	1,516	1,446	216	36	--
Chittenden	153	133	243	40	25	7	--	1,071	590	50	13	--
Rutland	602	433	520	51	132	2	1	1,318	840	334	85	2
Windham	428	756	577	461	152	4	0	1,609	2,122	279	51	--
Windsor	396	962	467	178	125	1	15	2,314	1,274	335	14	--
Total	2,064	2,796	2,789	858	610	18	18	8,853	6,865	1,281	224	2
Vermont total	4,052	5,894	7,185	940	1,449	130	18	24,192	16,579	1,855	330	73

[a] Includes only those counties that supplied pulpwood in 2006.

All table cells without observations are indicated by -- . Table value of 0 indicates the volume rounds to less than 1 standard cord, unpeeled.

Columns and rows may not add to their totals due to rounding.

Table 29.—Average production of active wood-pulp and composite product mills by company, location, and type of product produced, New England States, 2006

Product and company	Location	Product produced	Average production
Pulp mills			
Domtar Industries	Baileyville, Maine	Kraft pulp	1,450 tons pulp/day
Georgia-Pacific Corp.	Old Town, Maine	Kraft pulp	172 tons pulp/day
Katahdin Paper Company, LLC	East Millinocket, Maine	Groundwood/mechanical pulp	100 tons pulp/day
Knight Celotex Corporation	Farmington, Maine	Groundwood/mechanical pulp	100 tons pulp/day
Lincoln Paper And Tissue, LLC	Lincoln, Maine	Kraft pulp	450 tons pulp/day
Madison Paper Industries	Madison, Maine	Kraft pulp	300 tons pulp/day
Rumford Paper Company	Rumford, Maine	Kraft pulp	860 tons pulp/day
Sappi Fine Paper Company	Skowhegan, Maine	Kraft pulp	1,500 tons pulp/day
Verso Paper	Androscoggin, Maine	Kraft/groundwood pulp	1,570 tons pulp/day
Verso Paper	Bucksport, Maine	Groundwood/mechanical pulp	650 tons pulp/day
Fraser Paper	Berlin, New Hampshire	Sulfite pulp	650 tons pulp/day
Composite product mills			
Huber Engineered Woods, LLC	Easton, Maine	Oriented strand board	135 million ft^2, 3/4-inch basis per year
Louisiana-Pacific Corp.	Houlton, Maine	Oriented strand board	250 million ft^2, 3/4-inch basis per year

Table 30.—Other mills using Northern Region pulpwood in 2006
by company, location, and type of product produced

Company	Location	Product produced
Georgia-Pacific Corp.	Crossett, Arkansas	Sulfate pulp
Potlatch Corp.	McGehee, Arkansas	Sulfate pulp
NewPage Corp.	Wickliffe, Kentucky	Sulfate pulp
Weyerhaeuser Co.	Hawesville, Kentucky	Sulfate pulp
International Paper Co.	Riegelwood, North Carolina	Sulfate pulp
Georgia-Pacific Gypsum, LLC	Pryor, Oklahoma	Groundwood/mechanical pulp
International Paper Co.	Eastover, South Carolina	Sulfate pulp
Weyerhaeuser Co.	Kingsport, Tennessee	Soda and sulfite pulp
International Paper Co.	Franklin, Virginia	Sulfate pulp
MeadWestvaco Co.	Covington, Virginia	Sulfate pulp
St. Laurent Paperboard, Inc.	West Point, Virginia	Sulfate pulp
AV Cell, Inc.	Atholville, New Brunswick	Sulfate pulp
AV Nackowic, Inc.	Nackawic, New Brunswick	Kraft pulp
Fraser Paper	Edmundston, New Brunswick	Chemical/mechanical pulp
ATC Pembroke, Inc.	Pembroke, Ontario	Medium density fiberboard
Abitibi-Consolidated Co.	Thunder Bay, Ontario	Semichemical pulp
Abitibi-Consolidated Co.	Fort Frances, Ontario	Kraft/groundwod pulp
Bowater Canadian Forest Products	Thunder Bay, Ontario	Kraft pulp
Domtar, Inc.	Espanola, Ontario	Groundwood/mechanical pulp
Flakeboard Company Limited	Sault Ste. Marie, Ontario	Medium density fiberboard
St. Marys Paper, Ltd.	Sault Ste. Marie, Ontario	Groundwood/mechanical pulp
Domtar, Inc.	Windsor, Quebec	Kraft pulp
FPS Canada, Inc.	Thurso, Quebec	Kraft pulp
Kruger, Inc.	Trios-Rivieres, Quebec	Thermomechanical pulp

104

www.ingramcontent.com/pod-product-compliance
Lightning Source LLC
Chambersburg PA
CBHW081223280526
45787CB00006B/2501